BARRENLAND BEAUTIES

SHOWY PLANTS OF THE ARCTIC COAST

BY PAGE BURT

Outcrop Ltd
Yellowknife, Northwest Territories

Design: John Pekelsky
          Jean-Charles Dubé

Photographs: Page Burt (unless otherwise indicated)

Canadian Cataloguing in Publication Data

>   Burt, Page M., 1946-
>   Barrenland beauties
>
>   Text in English and Inuktitut.
>   Includes bibliographical references and index.
>   ISBN 0-919315-25-9
>
>   1. Botany--Arctic regions.   I. Title.
>   QK474.B88 1991   581.9719   C91-091713-2

Outcrop Ltd.
The Northern Publishers
Box 1350 Yellowknife, Northwest Territories
Canada X1A 2N9

Printed and bound in Canada

This book is dedicated to the
guests of Bathurst Inlet Lodge
and to the Kingaunmiut, the
people of the Nose mountain

Table of Contents

Foreword

In this volume, a veritable manual of arctic botany, Page Burt has produced a fascinating and descriptive introduction to the summer glory of arctic flower and plantlife in their misnamed habitat, the "Barrenlands." Page combines the expertise of a professional naturalist and the passion of a committed northerner, resulting in a work deserving wide attention. Both the amateur and professional botanist will find this introduction to the enormous variety of floral wonders a valued source of reference. However, they thereby expose themselves to that irresistable urge to go and see, in living color, these hardy beauties which survive and flourish each short summer in their arctic world.

Umani makpigagmi, nautiatiakhait naunaekhimangmata, nautiakhekhiyi Page Burt havakpaktuk ukuninga tiitigautigivlugit nautiakhaita takumaningit pakektauhimangmata nunaptingni ukiuktaktumi ilaani taiyauyuk "Pikangnngitpiaktumik." Una agnak, Page, nautkiakhekhiuyugami inuin nunanganik aliahuinakpakhuni uminga makpigaamik havayyagikpiaktuk. Aahin, kinalika uminga taigugumi nautianik kanuitilakhainik ilihimaniagunahiyuk ikayuktauvluni. Imaka kavlunak uminga taiguinakhuni inuin nunaanun akuiyumangniagunakhiyuk tautukuvlugit nautiat pinektun nautpangmata auyak tamana inungni.

John R. Sperry
Retired Bishop of the Arctic
Minihitakpak havaguekhimayuk inungni.

[Bishop Sperry spent 20 years as a minister in Coppermine, at a time when the Inuit still lived out on the land, in skin tents or igloos. He has travelled by dog team, on foot, and by small schooner and motorboat to the camps and places where people gathered to hunt, trap, or fish. As Anglican Bishop of the Arctic, he was responsible for the church along the entire arctic coast.]

Acknowledgements

Barrenland Beauties arose out of a need, in working with guests at Bathurst Inlet Lodge, to have some sort of reference book, with color pictures, to help visitors identify plants and remember plants they had seen. So, thanks must first go to the many guests at Bathurst Inlet Lodge over 19 summers, who stimulated me to learn the plants in order to interpret them.

Thanks, and credit for much of the substance of this book also should go to the Kingaunmiut, the people of Bathurst Inlet, especially Jessie Hagiolak Kapolak, John Nanagoak, Henry and Lena Kamoyoak, and Alice and Doris Kingnektak, for all the information so freely shared over so many years. Special thanks to the children, two generations of them, for sharing supplemental knowledge of uses of plants — some traditional, and some creative. (I'd *never* have thought of the use of new birch leaves as earrings!)

Several people played major roles in the development of this book. Sam Kapolak, of Bathurst Inlet, spent many hours photographing flowers. Susie Kapolak translated my material into Inuinaktun, working long into the winter nights, then proofreading, rewriting, and polishing her work. Margo Kadlun assisted Susie with some of the translation.

Thanks to Joanne Irons and Pat Thagard for contributing the sections on Coppermine and Cambridge Bay, and for the use of many photos, and to professional photographer David Middleton for the use of a number of his superb photos.

Bishop Sperry has been a constant inspiration, and was of great assistance in developing the section on the communities. Jon Woolf, of Cincinnati, assisted in the proofreading and typing of the Inuinaktun portion of the manuscript, and Pat Thagard, with the community section and final proofreading.

A special thanks to the team at Outcrop, and especially to Ronne Heming and Marion LaVigne, for putting up with all my procrastination and vacillation, and *still* being supportive.

My deepest appreciation to the Warner family of Bathurst Inlet Lodge for their constant and unswerving support of this project.

And thanks be to the land that brings forth such wonders, and does it again and again each year, with the coming of the arctic summer.

The writing and publication of Barrenland Beauties was made possible through an Economic Development Agreement grant to the Arctic Coast Tourist Association, and a grant from the Government of the Northwest Territories Department of Education.

Introduction

The arctic is a land of contrasts – a land of incomprehensible distances and awe-inspiring landforms, and a land of delicate, transient beauty.

Immense glacier-carved ridges, high rocky hills, ancient beaches, millions of lakes, and sparkling arctic rivers tumbling into dark gorges are part of the picture. On the coast and barrenlands, however, horizons recede into the far distance. Here the tundra stretches a thin green cape over the rocky skeleton of the land. Close up, in summer, the tundra becomes an exquisite oriental carpet, with dozens of species of flowers, all in a headlong rush to complete their cycles in a few brief weeks.

Compared to other biomes, the tundra is a simple system. Amateur botanists have a chance to learn a fair number of the local plants in a brief visit. The plants of the tundra are obvious, too – there's no forest to confuse and to occupy vertical space. Yet there are a lot of images; minute flowers, dwarf shrubs, and colorful lichens and mosses all jumbled together into a mosaic of intricate beauty. Simple though the system is, it is still complex enough to frustrate the casual visitor.

This book has been written to help the casual visitor identify the most common showy plants. Whether you are wandering around an arctic community or camped on the shores of an arctic river, we hope to provide some answers when you say, "I wonder what that little plant is called?".

Translations

For almost every species, there is a short section in Inuinaktun, which is the written form of the dialect commonly spoken in the central arctic. This is not a literal translation of the material in the species accounts, but a paraphrasing of the most important facts about a plant. In most of the central arctic the language is written in "Roman orthorgraphy", the alphabet familiar to Kablunak (non-Inuit).

Syllabics are used in the eastern part of the region. The dialect spoken by the Netslingmiut in the Gjoa Haven, Spence and Pelly Bay areas is quite different from that spoken by the Kitengmiut (the people of Victoria Island, Coppermine, and the Bathurst Inlet area).

Susie Kapolak, who grew up at Brown Sound in the Bathurst Inlet area, provided the translations. This was not an easy job, as few words in Inuinaktun deal with science, and spelling is only now being standardized. However, with the help of her mother, over the radio, she persisted, and later had her translations checked by a couple of interpreters. The idea was to provide information for residents who cannot read English.

Our apologies to the people of Gjoa Haven, Spence Bay and Pelly Bay, for not providing translations in syllabics. Funding and our knowledge of those areas did not permit these translations in this edition..

How to use this book

The species accounts are arranged in systematic order by their relation to other families (with minor exceptions). The layman who has some botanical knowledge may want to begin with a given family or group of families, and look up a species under that heading.

For those who'd prefer to begin with the flower color or shape, we've provided a key based on color, and an illustrated guide to shapes. In the key, all species of a given color are grouped together and subdivided by such characteristics as whether the flowers are regular (radially symmetrical, like buttercups, chickweeds, or cinquefoils), or irregular (bilaterally symmetrical, like the orchids, louseworts, or peas). These groupings are further divided using other characteristics, such as number of petals, and each genus or species listed has a few brief notes to help with identification. There are separate keys for trees and shrubs, and for berries, and one section for flowers that don't seem to fit anywhere else. If you haven't a clue as to what a plant is, sit down beside it, get out your hand lens, and run it through the key, gradually eliminating everything it is *not*.

A word of caution: This is a guide to the "showy" plants, and does not include all the species to be found in a particular area. Some groups (buttercups, chickweeds, dandelions) are quite complex, and have not received complete treatment. If you want to identify every flower in a given area, you will need a technical "flora". There are two for our area — Porsild and Cody's *Vascular Plants of the Continental Northwest Territories, Canada*, and Porsild's *Illustrated Flora of the Canadian Arctic Archipelago* (out of print, but available in libraries). The taxonomy in this guide follows that of Porsild and Cody (1980), so that this book can be used in conjunction with the larger flora. The floras do not have color illustrations, and require a working knowledge of botanical terms (though both have remarkably fine glossaries).

A Few Hints For Photographers

Arctic wildflowers are like minute jewels strewn about over the ground, precious in their very element of surprise. Although there are times when the ground is colored with flowers, it is far more common to find that you cannot see the flowers until you are within a few yards of an area. Then they burst into view, a myriad of colors and shapes, lending texture and pattern to a land that seems monochromatic when viewed from afar.

Photography of arctic wildflowers can be extremely rewarding, but very challenging. First, these flowers are small, some less than 1 cm across. Magnification is needed. A macro lens is useful, especially one that will provide 1:1 magnification. If you have no macro lens, there are a couple of less expensive alternatives.

Extension tubes can be placed between the lens and the camera. They place the lens farther from the film plane, thus making the image on the film plane larger. However, using extension tubes causes less light to strike the film plane, thus reducing the effective speed of the lens.

Close-up magnifying rings are an inexpensive alternative. They screw on the front of the lens, magnifying the image. They do not significantly reduce the amount of light reaching the film plane, unless all three are stacked. However, they do add pieces of glass between the subject and the film plane. The more lenses between subject and film plane, the more degradation of the image.

In some cases, you can use a combination of the above equipment, and even some other combinations, like linking two lenses, or using telextenders or extension tubes with telephoto lenses. Experiment during the winter to find the best combination for your needs. Work with small flowers from a florist to try out various combinations, so you don't waste dollars on unsatisfactory combinations.

The most useful piece of equipment for sharp photos is a tripod, beanbag, or some method of stabilizing your camera. With a tripod, you will need to use a cable release to trip the shutter, so you don't add camera motion with the pressure of your finger.

A small flash system, mounted on an adjustable bracket that puts the flash at the same distance from the subject as the prime lens, will enable you to achieve maximum depth of field by allowing you to use the smallest aperture on your camera. (This method is described in John Shaw's books.)

No matter what system you use, you will have two additional problems, problems with depth of field, and problems with motion due to wind. Both these problems can be solved in several ways, but it was not my intention to write a book on flower photography, so I will refer readers to the following three superb books on the subject:

Shaw, John. 1984. *Nature Photographer's Complete Guide to Professional Field Techniques.* Amphoto, New York

Shaw, John. 1987. *Close-ups in Nature.* Amphoto, New York

Blacklock, Craig and Nadine. 1987. *Photographing Wildflowers.* Voyageur Press, Stillwater, Minn.

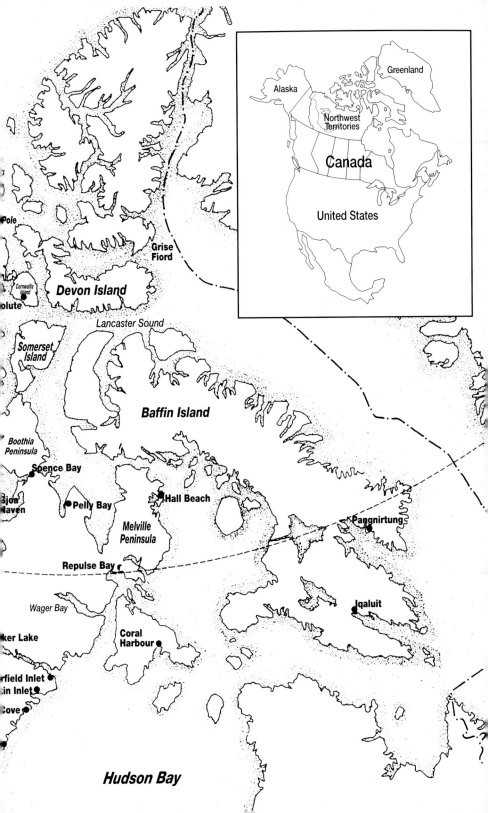

Pole

Grise
Fiord

Cornwallis
Island

olute

Devon Island

Lancaster Sound

*Somerset
Island*

Baffin Island

*Boothia
Peninsula*

Spence Bay

ăjoa
Haven

Pelly Bay

Hall Beach

Pangnirtung

*Melville
Peninsula*

Repulse Bay

Wager Bay

Iqaluit

ker Lake

**Coral
Harbour**

rfield Inlet
in Inlet

Cove

Hudson Bay

Alaska

Greenland

Northwest
Territories

Canada

United States

BARRENLAND
BEAUTIES

Color and Shape

- · Yellow Flowers
- · Blue to Purple Flowers
- · Pink, Red to Magenta Flowers
- · White Flowers
- · Berries or Fruit
- · Trees & Shrubs
- · Lichens
- · Odd Stuff

Color and Shape
A key to plants in this guide

The species accounts are arranged systematically, under their particular plant families. The flowers in a family or genus, or species, may occur in several different colors, making it difficult to find a given flower. Most people first look at the color, THEN look at other characteristics.

This key will help you locate plants in this guide first by color, then by readily identifiable or special characteristics.

You will need to be familiar with a few plant terms, such as *regular* or *irregular* flowers, *basal* or *stem* leaves, *palmately* or *pinnately compound*, *stamen, pistil, sepal*, etc. These words are in the Glossary in the back of the book — look them up as you come to them. It may also help to have a hand-lens to magnify the blooms of the flower you are identifying. To save space, commonly used terms have been abbreviated: *plant* = *pl.*; *flower* = *fl.*; *flowerhead* = *flrhd.*; leaves = *lvs.* Color terms refer to flower color.

Locate the section referring to the color of your flower, and then read all sub-sections under it. If one fits, try the short descriptions for each flower. These will eliminate all but a couple. Look those up by page number.

There are separate keys to berries, and shrubs over 30 cm in height.

YELLOW FLOWERS

(INCLUDING FLOWERS THAT ARE ALMOST YELLOW)

 ## Irregular Flowers

FALSE ASPHODEL, *Tofieldia pusilla.* Greenish-yellow, tight cluster, parts difficult to discern. p. 38

NORTHERN BOG ORCHID, *Habenaria obtusata.* Yellowish-green; single basal leaf w/parallel veins. p. 42

CORAL-ROOT ORCHID, *Corallorhiza trifida.* Brownish-yellow; no leaves, lacks chlorophyll. p. 42

YELLOW OXYTROPE, *Oxytropis maydelliana.* Pea fl., light yellow. p. 120

LOUSEWORTS, *Pedicularis*, spp. Flowers with helmet, borne on spike.

HEADED LOUSEWORT, *Pedicularis capitata.* Pale yellow, 2-4 fl. in short head. p. 172

LAPLAND LOUSEWORT, *Pedicularis lapponica.* Pale yellow, stalk unbranched. p. 172

LABRADOR LOUSEWORT, *Pedicularis labradorica.* Light yellow, stem branched. p. 174

FLAME LOUSEWORT, *Pedicularis flammea.* Yellow, with red on helmet; red stem, very small. p. 172

 Regular Flowers
Flowers in capitate "head", composite family

WORMWOOD, *Artemisia* sp. Yellowish-green, small flrhds.; foliage aromatic. p. 188

ALPINE ARNICA, *Arnica alpina.* Bright yellow, lvs. opposite. p. 182

DANDELION, *Taraxacum* sp. Bright yellow, all ray fl.; basal rosette, toothed lvs. p. 196

DWARF HAWKSBEARD, *Crepis nana.* Bright yellow, all ray fl.; basal rosette, dwarf. p. 192

MASTODON FLOWER, *Senecio congestus.* Bright yellow; plant hairy. p. 196

GROUNDSEL, *Senecio atropurpureus.* Bright yellow; all disk fl., or both ray fl. and disk fl. present. p. 194

BLACK-TIPPED GROUNDSEL, *Senecio lugens.* Bright yellow, ray and disk fl., 5-12 heads per stalk. p. 194

 Flowers with 4 petals, arranged in cross shape

YELLOW WALLFLOWER, *Erysimum inconspicuum.* Light yellow, tight terminal raceme. p. 70

TANSY-MUSTARD, *Descurainia sophioides.* Fl. very small, light yellow, fernlike leaves. p. 72

ARCTIC BLADDERPOD, *Lesquerella arctica.* Fl. in racemes of 5-9 fl., which may have 5-7 petals; spatulate lvs. in basal rosette, grey foilage, stellate hairs. p. 74

 Flowers with 5 petals

ARCTIC POPPY, *Papaver radicatum.* Yellow w/ greenish tint; seeds in hairy capsule. p. 84

YELLOW MOUNTAIN SAXIFRAGE, *Saxifraga azoides.* Bright yellow, orange dots toward tip of petals; succulent lvs. p. 110

YELLOW MARSH SAXIFRAGE, *Saxifrage hirculus.* Yellow w/orange dots in rows toward base of petal. p. 110

SHRUBBY CINQUEFOIL, *Potentilla fruticosa*. Bright yellow; shrub, reddish brown peeling bark. p. 90

SEASIDE CINQUEFOIL, *Potentilla egedii*. Bright yellow; lvs. pinnately compound; red stolons. p. 90

SNOW CINQUEFOIL, *Potentilla nivea*. Bright yellow; lvs. w. 3 leaflets, white hairs; tall. p. 92

 Flowers with 5, 6, or more petals, petaloid sepals or petals and colored sepals.

RICHARDSON'S ANEMONE, *Anemone richardsonii*. Bright yellow sepals, no petals; lvs. in whorl on stem. p. 78

MARSH MARIGOLD, *Caltha palustris*. Bright yellow, lvs. reniform. p. 80

YELLOW WATER CROWFOOT, *Ranunculus gmelinii*. Light yellow; lvs. 5-parted, notched; submerged/emergent. p. 82

NORTHERN BUTTERCUP, *Ranunculus pedatifidus*. Shiny yellow; stem lvs. sessile, 3-lobed. p. 84

DWARF BUTTERCUP, *Ranunculus pygmaeus*. Shiny yellow; basal lvs. 3-lobed, notched; pl. tiny. p. 84

ARCTIC BLADDERPOD, *Lesquerella arctica*. Fl. yellow, in racemes of 5-9 fl., each can have 5-7 petals; lvs. greyish, spatulate, in basal rosette; stellate hairs. p. 74

BLUE TO PURPLE FLOWERS

 ## Irregular Flowers

BUTTERWORT, *Pinguicula* sp. Purplish-blue fl. with spur; yellowish lvs. in basal rosette. p. 150

ARCTIC LUPINE, *Lupinus arcticus*. Bright blue-and-white pea; lvs. palmately compound. p. 114

BEACH-PEA, *Lathyrus japonicus*. Lt. blue to purple; lvs. pinnately-cmpd., with tendrils. p. 118

ALPINE MILK-VETCH, *Astragalus alpinus*. Lt. blue w/purple streaking, pea; lvs. pinnate cmpd. p. 116

ARCTIC CRAZYWEED, *Oxytropis arctica*. Pea, pink/magenta to bluish purple (esp on arctic islands), lvs. pin. cmpd.; foliage green. p. 122

Oxytropis arctobia. Peas, pink/magenta to blue/purple, lvs. pin. cmpd.; low, grey foliage. p. 122

Regular Flowers
Flowers in compact head, composite family

SIBERIAN ASTER, *Aster sibericus.* Bluish ray fl., yellow disk fl.; lvs. w/ serrate margins. p. 184

PYGMY ASTER, *Aster pygmaeus.* Bluish ray-fl., yellow disk-fl.; lvs. narrow, entire margins. p. 184

FIREWORKS FLOWER, *Saussurea angustifolia.* Purple, w/white tips, disk fl. only; 3-5 flrhds .in terminal cluster. p. 192

Flowers with 5 distinct petals, not fused

PURPLE MOUNTAIN SAXIFRAGE, *Saxifraga oppositifolia.* Bluish to purplish; lvs. opposite, reduced; pl. prostrate. p. 108

STAR GENTIAN, *Lomatogonium rotatum.* Sky-blue, with darker sepals; stem/lvs. reddish green. p. 148

FLAX, *Linum lewisii.* Light blue, loose leafy raceme; lvs. linear; several flowering stems per plant. p. 156

PRIMROSE, *Primula stricta.* White, occas. lavender, yellow "eye" in centre, petals fused at base; 2-5 fl. in small umbel; basal rosette. p. 162

Flowers with petals fused into tube or bell-like structure

PURPLE BLADDER-CAMPION, *Melandrium apetalum.* Purple calyx inflated, translucent, streaked, nodding. p. 62

ARCTIC HAREBELL, *Campanula uniflora.* Light blue, open bell, nodding; lvs. alternate. p. 152

Gentiana propinqua. Blue to purplish, petals fused at bases, lobes bristle-tipped; foliage purplish green. p. 146

Gentiana tenella. Light blue; foliage lt. green. p. 146

SEASIDE BLUEBELL, *Mertensia maritima.* Light blue (pink when young); plant prostrate, grey-green fleshy leaves. p. 148

PRIMROSE, *Primula stricta.* Usually white, sometimes lavender, fused at bases into tube, yellow "eye", 3-5 fl. in umbel; basal rosette, p. 162

PINK · RED TO MAGENTA FLOWERS

 ## Irregular Flowers

PAINTBRUSH, *Castilleja* spp. Fl. hidden behind pink to magenta colored bracts; lvs. narrow, lanceolate. p. 168

ARCTIC LOUSEWORT, *Pedicularis arctica.* Pink, small tooth on helmet. p. 172

WOOLLY LOUSEWORT, *Pedicularis lanata.* Pink; helmet lacks tooth, hairy stem; taproot lemon-yellow. p. 174

SUDETAN LOUSEWORT, *Pedicularis sudetica.* Magenta helmet, light pink lower lip w/magenta dots, short spike. p. 176

RICHARDSON'S MILK-VETCH, *Astragalus richardsonii.* Pea, pink/magenta with creamy white, keel purplish tipped. p. 116

BEACH-PEA, *Lathyrus japonicus.* Pea, color varies pink to magenta to blue; lvs. pinnately compound, with tendrils. p.118

ARCTIC CRAZYWEED, *Oxytropis arctica.* Pea, bright pink w/white blaze on standard, bluish purple on arctic islands, fragrant. p. 122

Oxytropis arctobia. Pea, pink to bluish purple; low grey-matted foliage. p. 122

LIQUORICE-ROOT, *Hedysarum alpinum.* Pea, pink, unscented; in long raceme, fl. all to one side. p. 118

NORTHERN SWEET-PEA, *Hedysarum mackenzeii.* Pea, bright magenta, very fragrant; in short loose raceme. p. 118/120

 ## Regular Flowers
Flowers with 3 petals (or multiples of 3)

WILD CHIVES, *Allium schoenoprasum.* Purplish-pink, globular umbel; oniony smell. p. 40

REDDISH FALSE ASPHODEL, *Tofieldia coccinea.* Pink to dark red fl. in short tight spike; lvs. clasping, flattened laterally. p. 38

 ### *Flowers with 4 petals, in cross shape*

PALLAS' WALLFLOWER, *Erysimum pallasii.* Purplish-pink fl. in globular raceme, fragrant; lvs. linear-lanceolate, basal and stem lvs. p. 68

TALL FIREWEED, *Epilobium angustifolium.* Light magenta, narrow dark pink sepals between wide petals, 3-3.5 cm.; lvs. linear. p. 154

DWARF FIREWEED, *Epilobium latifolium.* Light magenta, narrow dark sepals alt. with petals, grey-green, fleshy leaves. p. 154

 ## *Flowers with 5 petals*

MOSS-CAMPION, *Silene acaulis.* Bright reddish-pink, petals basally fused into tube; cushion plant. p. 64

PURPLE MOUNTAIN SAXIFRAGE, *Saxifraga oppositifolia.* Bluish to purplish; lvs. opposite, reduced, prostrate. p. 108

MARSH FIVE-FINGER, *Potentilla palustris.* Dark reddish-purple, 2 cm, petals shorter than sepals; foliage reddish-green; amphibious. p. 92

ALPINE AZALEA, *Loiseleuria procumbens.* Fl. small, pink to white w/red pedicels; foliage low, matted. p. 140

LAPLAND ROSEBAY, *Rhododendron lapponicum.* Bright pink/purple, fragrant; dwarf shrub w/ovate lvs. p. 134

THRIFT, *Armeria maritima.* Pink globular clusters, each fl. set in cup formed by papery bracts, lvs. linear, basal. p. 144

 ## *Flowers bladder- or urn-shaped*

PURPLE BLADDER-CAMPION, *Melandrium apetalum.* Reddish-purple, nodding, w/inflated translucent calyx. p. 62

BOG ROSEMARY, *Andromeda polifolia.* Pink urns on long pedicels, nodding; dwarf shrub, linear-lanceolate lvs.. p. 130

BLUEBERRY, *Vaccinium uliginosum.* Red to pink urn-to-bell-shaped fl.; small shrub, lvs. oval, dull green. p. 136

LINGONBERRY, *Vaccinium vitis-idaea.* Reddish pink to white urn-shaped flowers, prostrate shrub, lvs. shiny, oval, grooved. p. 138

 ## Flowers Indeterminate

CROWBERRY, *Empetrum nigrum.* Minute red fl., in axils of terminal lvs.; lvs. linear, 5 mm; prostrate mats. p. 126

MOUNTAIN SORREL, *Oxyria digyna.* Red to reddish-green, in racemes, seedpods reddish, flat; lvs. reniform, fleshy. p. 58

REDDISH FALSE ASPHODEL, *Tofieldia coccinea.* Pink to dark red flowers in short, tight spike; leaves parallel-veined, linear, clasping. p. 38

WHITE FLOWERS

 ## Flowers Irregular

PAINTED-CUP, *Castilleja,* spp. Yellowish-white, creamy to pinkish bracts concealing the true flowers. p. 168

Occasionally, you will find white forms of the louseworts, lupines, or lapland rosebay.

 ## Flowers Regular
Flowers in tight "heads", composites

RAY FLOWERS WHITE, DISK FLOWERS YELLOW
FLEABANE, *Erigeron* spp. Narrow white ray fl.; involucral bracts and stem hairy. p. 186

WILD CHAMOMILE, *Matricaria ambigua.* Lvs. fernlike. p. 186

ARCTIC DAISY, *Chrysanthemum integrifolium.* Lvs. linear, basal rosette. p. 184

RAY AND DISC FLOWERS WHITE
YARROW, *Achillea nigrescens.* Flhds. creamy white, in tight corymb; lvs. fernlike, alternate, aromatic. p. 180

COLTSFOOT, *Petasites* spp. Flrhds. of white to pinkish flat-topped clusters of 4-10 flrhds.; lvs. large, coarsely-toothed. p. 190

PUSSY-TOES, *Antennaria* spp. Dense cluster (ray flrs. lacking), basal rosette. p. 182

 Flowers in tight spike or head; difficult to count petals

FALSE ASPHODEL, *Tofieldia pusilla.* Greenish-white, parts in multiples of 3, short spike, lvs. parallel veined, basal. p. 38

BISTORT, *Polygonum viviparum.* Flrs. w/prominent stamens, lower fl. replaced by bulbils; leaves linear, sheaths at joints. p. 58

Flowers with 4 petals, in cross shape

SCURVY-GRASS, *Cochlearia officinalis.* Sm. fl. w/ widely separated petals; leaves spoon-shaped, fleshy, w/long petioles. p. 70

Draba glabella. Bright white, in 5-15 fl. raceme; basal and stem lvs. soft hairy, variable. p. 74

CUCKOO FLOWER, *Cardamine pratensis.* White to lavender, 1-1.5 cm, 5-10 in flat-topped raceme, petals 3x the length of sepals; lvs. pinnately compound, many leaflets. p. 72

BITTER CRESS, *Cardamine digitata.* Milky white, .4-.8 cm, in elongating raceme, petals 2x the length of sepals; leaves with 5-7 pinnate leaflets, p. 72

PARRYA, *Parrya arctica.* Fl. creamy white to lavender, 1-1.5 cm, 7-12 in wide raceme; lvs. lanceolate, basal rosette. Rare in our area, so not in species accounts. p. 68

Flowers with inflated calyx or petals fused in urn or bell shape

BLADDER-CAMPION, *Melandrium affine.* 5 white petals at apex of inflated striped calyx, p. 62

BEARBERRY, *Arctostaphylos* spp. Greenish white, urn-shaped, blooming before lvs. fully emerge. p. 132

LINGONBERRY, *Vaccinium vitis-idaea.* White to pinkish, urn-shaped, 2-5 in cluster at tips of prostrate branches. p. 138

WHITE ARCTIC HEATHER, *Cassiope tetragona.* White bells on long arching pedicels; leaves small, dark green, four-ranked. p. 130

SIDE-FLOWERED WINTERGREEN, *Pyrola secunda.* Yellowish/greenish white, tight urns, pistil protruding, flrs. on side of scape; lvs. along lower part of stem. p. 158

Flowers with 5 petals (or petaloid sepals), not obviously fused

LEAVES OPPOSITE;
FLOWERS WITH DEEPLY NOTCHED OR DIVIDED PETALS
STAR CHICKWEED, *Stellaria* sp. Petals so deeply notched they look divided. p. 60

MOUSE-EAR CHICKWEED, *Cerastium alpinum.* Deeply-notched petals; leaves and stem hairy. p. 60

LEAVES OPPOSITE; FLOWERS WITH UNDIVIDED PETALS
SEABEACH SANDWORT, *Honckenya peploides.* Greenish-white, ovate petals, sepals longer than petals; leaves fleshy, on beaches. p. 64

PLANTS WITH BASAL ROSETTES; ONE FLOWER PER SCAPE
GRASS-OF-PARNASSUS, *Parnassia* sp. Large fl. (2 - 2.5 cm), petals wider than long; stamens alt. with staminodea; light green spoon-shaped leaves, p. 98

BULBLET SAXIFRAGE, *Saxifraga cernua.* Fl. 1.5 - 2 cm), petals longer than wide; reddish bulblets along stem; basal leaves with 5 - 7 lobes, p. 104

PLANTS WITH BASAL ROSETTES; FLOWERS IN UMBELS (Primroses)
PRIMROSE, *Primula stricta.* Fl. in umbel of 3-6, petals notched, yellow "eye" in centre of flower; rosette of green basal leaves, p. 162

ROCK-JASMINE, *Androsace chaemojasmae.* Few-fl. umbel, petals not notched, fragrant, fl. 8-10 mm; basal rosette of small, hairy leaves, p. 162

FAIRY CANDELABRA, *Androsace septentrionalis.* Umbel of 4 to many fl., petals not notched, flrs. 4-6 mm; scape and basal rosette reddish-green, p. 164

 Plants with basal rosettes;
flowers in raceme or panicle

BASAL LEAVES WITH DISTINCT PETIOLES
BULBLET SAXIFRAGE, *Saxifraga cernua.* Single fl.; red bulblets along stem; lvs. with 5-7 lobes. p. 104

HEART-LEAVED SAXIFRAGE, *Saxifraga punctata.* Fl. in loose raceme, 2 styles, reddish, diverging; lvs. with long petioles, 12-14 lobes, p. 106

BROOK SAXIFRAGE, *Saxifraga rivularis.* 1-3 fl. in raceme, styles not obvious; lvs. with 3-5 lobes. p. 108

LARGE-FLOWERED WINTERGREEN, *Pyrola grandiflora.* Waxy white fl., 12 mm across, fragrant, on short reddish pedicels; leaves oval, leathery, with waxy surface, p. 158

SIDE-FLOWERED WINTERGREEN, *Pyrola secunda.* Greenish white urn-shaped fl. of 5 petals; all fl. on same side of scape, p. 158

BASAL LEAVES WITHOUT DISTINCT PETIOLES
SNOW SAXIFRAGE, *Saxifraga nivalis.* Fl. white, styles red, in tight panicle; undersides of basal leaves purple, p. 104

PRICKLY SAXIFRAGE, *Saxifraga tricuspidata.* Fl. w/spots on petals, 3-10 in cluster; basal leaves straplike, with three prickly points, p. 106

WITH BASAL LEAVES, BUT NOT DISTINCT ROSETTE; SINGLE FLOWER
FEW-FLOWERED ANEMONE, *Anemone parviflora.* Fl. w/white sepals, no petals, faint blue blush on back of sepals; stem lvs. 3-lobed, basal lvs. w/3 leaflets, p. 80

SMALL SHRUBS; FLOWERS IN UMBEL-LIKE CLUSTER
LABRADOR TEA, *Ledum decumbens.* Fl. in umbel-like clusters, 10-20 per cluster; small shrub, narrow aromatic lvs., p. 134

PLANT FORMING LOW MAT, FLOWERS LARGE
Diapensia lapponica. Fl. on stiff pedicels above low mat (or cushion); lvs. narrowly spatulate, p. 160

LEAVES LARGE, MAPLE-LIKE; FLOWERS LARGE
CLOUDBERRY, *Rubus chamaemorus.* Fl. solitary, large (2-3.5 cm); 1-3 large 5-lobed lvs. with serrate margins; produces yellow berry, p. 94

 Flowers with 8 - 10 petals

MOUNTAIN AVENS, *Dryas integrifolia.* Fl. large (2.5-3.5 cm); lvs. lanceolate-oblong, dark green above, white beneath, p. 86

 # *PLANTS PRODUCING BERRIES OR EDIBLE FRUIT*
KEYED BY COLOR OF RIPE BERRIES.

Berries Black

CROWBERRY, *Empetrum nigrum.* Small (1 cm) black berries with 4 big seeds, in tight groups (1-5 per group) at ends of prostrate twigs w/short, narrow leaves. p. 126

BLACK BEARBERRY, *Arctostaphylos alpina.* Large (1.5 cm) black berries at base of spatulate leaves. p. 132

Berries Blue

BLUEBERRY, *Vaccinium uliginosum.* Medium-sized (.75-1.5) cm blue berries w/whitish "bloom" on surface, on low shrubs; lvs. ovate, dull green. p. 136

Berries Red/Orange

SOAPBERRIES, *Shepherdia canadensis.* Shiny red-orange berries (1 cm) with raised speckles. p. 128

RED BEARBERRY, *Arctostaphylos rubra.* Large (1.5 cm) translucent red berry at base of spatulate leaves. p. 132

KINNIKINICK, *Arctostaphylos uvi-ursi.* Medium (1 cm) mealy orange berries; ovate yellowish leathery leaves, evergreen; fl. white with pink margin to petals, urn-shaped. Rare in our area, so not in species accounts.

LINGONBERRY, *Vaccinium vitis-idaea*. Small (75 mm) red berries maturing to maroon color; in clusters of 1-6 at tips of branches; leaves shiny, grooved, ovate. p. 138

BOG CRANBERRY, *Oxycoccus microcarpus*. Small (75 mm) dark red berries borne on trailing branches of small prostrate shrubs, in sphagnum moss; fl. pink, petals reflexed. Rare in our area, so not in species accounts.

Berries Yellow

CLOUDBERRY, *Rubus chamaemorus*. Large (1.5-2 cm) soft, raspberry-like fruit, solitary on stem, red, then salmon, then yellow; 1-3 palmately-lobed leaves. p. 94

TREES/SHRUBS · WOODY PLANTS OVER 30 CM TALL

Leaves Compound

SHRUBBY CINQUEFOIL, *Potentilla fruticosa*. Lvs. palmately compound, with 5 linear leaflets; reddish peeling bark; fl. large (2-3 cm), bright yellow, p. 90

Leaves Simple

LEAVES OPPOSITE

SOAPBERRY, *Shepherdia canadensis*. Lvs. ovate, almost always opposite, dark green above, silvery below; red-orange berries. p. 128

LEAVES ALTERNATE

WILLOWS, *Salix* sp. Lvs. linear, ovate; dioecious plants, catkins upright, not drooping, p. 48

DWARF BIRCH, *Betula glandulosa*. Lvs. ovate, 1-2 cm, w/ rounded serrations on margin; monoecious plants with staminate and pistillate catkins, p. 54

GREEN ALDER, *Alnus crispa*. Lvs. broadly ovate, 5-8 cm, dark green and shiny on upper surface, with finely serrated margin; monoecious plants with drooping pendulous male catkins, and upright, woody female catkins which resemble miniature pine cones, p. 52

There are several other woody shrubs, such as the blueberries, cranberries, crowberry, heather, Lapland rosebay, moss campion, and *Diapensia* but these are all less than 30 cm in height, so are not included in this key. They will key out under flower color.

LICHENS

A few lichens are described and illustrated in this book, but it is by no means anything more than a sampling of a few common and obvious species. Turn to the section on lichens, and match specimens to the photos to identify. For lichen identification, which is a complicated affair, we recommend Vitt, Marsh, and Bovey's (1988) *Mosses, Lichens, and Ferns of Northwest North America*. The Dept. of Indian and Northern Affairs has also printed a looseleaf guide to the lichens of the Northwest Territories, which is quite useful. It is (1991) available from D.I.A.N.D., P.O. Box 1500, in Yellowknife.

ODD STUFF!

These don't fit easily into any regular categories, such as flower color, woody vs. non-woody, etc.

Ferns, emerging as coiled fiddleheads

FRAGRANT SHIELD FERN, *Dryopteris fragrans*. Fronds dry and somewhat leathery, twice- or thrice-pinnate, dark green, lacking indusia over the sori, p. 26

FRAGILE FERN, *Cystopteris fragilis*. Fronds shiny and somewhat translucent, twice- or thrice pinnate, bright green, with hood-like indusium over the sori, p. 26

WOODSIA, *Woodsia glabella*. Fronds thin, delicate, once-pinnate, yellowish green, usually less than 15 cm, indusia attached under the sori. Not common in our area, so not included in the species accounts.

Small "birdsnests" with leafy collar

GOLDEN SAXIFRAGE, *Chrysosplenium tetrandrum*. Very odd, dwarf plant without petals, sepals yellowish-green, leaves forming a collar just under the flowers, seeds borne in small cups. p. 100

Upright stems, like bottle brushes

CLUB-MOSSES, *Lycopodium* sp. Small, dry plants with upright bristly branches, producing spores in terminal conelike strobili or small strobili in axils of upper leaves, p. 30

COMMON HORSETAIL, *Equisetum arvense*. To 30 cm, upright rod-like stems, jointed, with branches in whorl at nodes; spores borne on separate fertile fronds which lack chlorophyll, p. 28

MARE'S TAIL, *Hippuris vulgaris*. Aquatic-emergent, single stems with whorls of leaves, inconspicuous flowers borne in axils of upper whorls, p. 44

Single upright stems, with or without slender leaves

VARIEGATED HORSETAIL, *Equisetum variegatum*. Small, slender stems, some prostrate, some vertical, minute straplike leaves at nodes in whorls, bicolored, p. 28

ARCTIC COTTON, *Eriophorum* sp. Flowering heads silky white tufts; leaves narrow, linear, with closed sheaths, either tussock-forming or growing individually, p. 36

GRASSES, family Graminae. Only a couple of the grasses have been included in this book, p. 34. The grasses are very important, but in most cases are not showy, and require a specialized vocabulary to identify. See Porsild and Cody (1980) for keys to the grasses.

Greyish catkins, on tiny woody plants

NET-VEINED WILLOW, *Salix reticulata*. Prostrate, dioecious; upright catkins with stamens & pistils emerging from hairs along stem. p. 50

LEAST WILLOW, *Salix herbacea*. Prostrate, minute; p. 52

DWARF BIRCH, *Betula glandulosa*. Prostrate, p. 54

NOTES:

Jewel Lichen *Xanthoria elegans*

Lichens, Ferns, Horsetails, Club-Mosses

- Jewel lichen
  Xanthoria elegans
- Rock tripe
  Umbilicaria, sp.
- Antler lichen
  Masonhalea richardsonii
- Worm lichen
  Thamnolia subuliformis sp.
- Map lichen
  Rhizocarpon geographicum
- Sunburst lichen
  Arctoparmelia centrifuga
- Fragrant shield fern
  Dryopteris fragrans
- Fragile fern
  Cystopteris fragilis
- Horsetail
  Equisetum arvense
- Club-mosses
  Lycopodium sp.

LICHENS · KAGIUYAT

Take a close look at the tundra, and you will be amazed at the variety of lichens. These fascinating plants were once thought to be an excellent example of "symbiosis", or cooperative interaction between two very different plants — a fungus and an alga (Vitt, Marsh, & Bovey, 1988). The algal cells carry on photosynthesis, utilizing sunlight to produce food, especially sugar alcohols, which it supplies to the fungal partner. The role of the fungus is not clearly understood; it was originally thought it absorbed and held moisture, which allowed the alga to grow and reproduce.

However, scientists are now not so sure. Many now feel that the interrelationship between the algae and the fungus seems to be a finely-controlled parasitism in which the fungus is parasitic on the alga. Somehow the alga seems to balance the death of algal cells with the production of new cells. The alga does not seem to benefit much, if at all. In fact, most of the species of algae that are involved in lichens also are free-living. It's almost as though the lichen-forming fungi are able to capture the algae and put them to use to form a lichen ... But there's still a lot that is not known about these odd plant associations.

Lichens make up a substantial part of the summer diet of caribou. Musk oxen occasionally feed on them, and they play an important role in the plant colonization process on stable rocks or old beaches. Ancient beaches, at sea level during the Pleistocene, have risen with the land in an process called "glacial rebound". Now hundreds of feet above sea level, many of these gravel beaches consist of wave-rounded stones webbed together by lichens. They are part of a succession of plant communities that changes over time. The lichen community stabilizes the gravel, and rooted flowering plants can become established. Each plant community contributes to the humus (organic material) in the old beach, gradually building a soil that can support more and more species of plants.

Lichens are more sensitive to certain types of air pollution than are other plants. They can provide an index to air pollution near urban areas and are studied for this purpose in many parts of the world.

Since the lichens are not covered in Porsild and Cody's *Vascular Plants of the Continental Northwest Territories, Canada*, we have followed the taxonomy in use in Vitt, Marsh and Bovey's *Mosses, Lichens, and Ferns of Northwest North America*, as it seems to be readily available, and the range maps cover most of our area.

Kagiuyat (all lichens are kagiuyat in Inuinaktun)

Kagiuyat kuyaginak nunami naotiyukton. Oyakani naoyokton, hanainilo hinani oyakani, naotianilo naokataoyokton. Mingotiton iliyukton, nuyaktonlonit, imohimayutolonit tetegak, algihimayutotlonit keyok.

Kagiuyat alginaton atongaoyat. Kagiuyat amigaiton allatkitaton, hapkoat malgonik naojutilgik, aipa imaitomik pilik chlorophyll, ima ona nekeliuyuktok, onataot aipagiya fungus, imaton ona naotiagota, imalo atipkaohimajuta naotiligangamik, aipalonit nekegivata. Naotialikiut naonaitaiyuitait.

Amigaitot allatkit kagiuyat. Ekiton teteganiaktakon.

Lichen tundra

Jewel Lichen
Xanthoria elegans

A bright orange lichen which grows flatly, close to the rock. It is abundant on calcareous rocks (those rich in carbonate compounds, such as the limestones and dolomites). It is also an indicator of high nitrogen content, growing on non-calcareous rocks which have been covered with years of accumulated whitewash (from perching birds), on mammal lookout posts or where animals urinate frequently (ground squirrel, pika, and marmot posts). It is possible to fly along cliffs, and locate traditional hawk and falcon nesting sites from an aircraft, just by looking for spots where this colorful lichen is abundant. The very similar lichens in the genus *Caloplaca* are also common on calcareous rock, but are more crustose. They are difficult to distinguish from *Xanthoria*.

Jewel Lichen Ona piniktok aolaosigalik kagiuyak naonaitok, imaitokanikmi calciumi naoyuktok. Hongayatoni oyakani naotiyukton, oyakanilo kopanoat anakviini, hogatlonit hitigavigaloani, hamanilo hogat kiokataviini, naotiayukhivagamik nakogigamigit huna taimailigangami.

Rock Tripe
Umbilicaria, sp.

These are the black leathery-looking lichens adhering to many rocks in our area, growing best on non-calcareous rocks, often on surfaces with high glacial polish.

On their trek across the Barrens from the Hood River to Fort Enterprise, the starving men of the Franklin expedition of 1819-1822 attempted to eat these lichens. As a result, nausea and diarrhea further weakened them — the lichens contained not only rock particles, but also high levels of acids, which irritated their digestive tracts. (Boiling in several changes of water, with the addition of baking soda, would have made them edible, but Franklin's men lacked the fuel, the time, and the baking soda.)

Rock Tripe Ona kingnagitok kagiuyak naotiyukton oyakani, ilani allatkitlo naogatigiyutait. Ona Sir John Franklin aolaoyakpaktok nunaoyaliuhonilo nunaptini 1821 - 22 milo ilangitaok avonga Katimanakmi avonga Winter Lakemot aolakpaton. Aolaktilogit akiagoakayakton. Nekehaigamik ona kagiuyak pokohogit oyakamit, kitolihakhogo hehaitomot imakmon negevaktat.

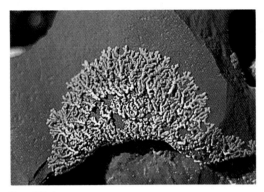

Jewel Lichen

Rock Tripe *Umbilicaria*, sp.

Antler Lichen
Masonhalea richardsonii

Also called "tumbleweed lichen", this foliose lichen grows unattached and is blown about by the wind, collecting in depressions in the tundra. When wet, it becomes pliable and unrolls, closely resembling miniature antlers of caribou or moose. One side is dark brown, and the other, grey with oval brown spots.

Antler Lichen Tokhoaton itot ona kuyaginak naoyukton nunami. Takohoalikpaton hapkoak tuktuton nakyuiton itot. Hapkoak maklongayut kagiuyan, katinilikton ikloa. Nunamon atangiton, anokimi titkatayukton.

Worm Lichen
Thamnolia subuliformis

This lichen grows in loosely attached groups in the vegetative mat of the tundra and resembles a bunch of worms crawling over each other. The hollow white, sometimes branched, tubelike stalks are easily recognized. It probably reproduces by pieces of the thallus (hollow tubes) breaking off, blowing away, and continuing to grow.

Worm Lichen Ona kakoktak kagiuyak nunaptini naoyukton. Allatkiktahotik hapkoa naoyukton. Amogokni ona takohongoyat iloa tohoatot itot. Ahigogangami tikatanin allamik naotkiyukton.

Map Lichen
Rhizocarpon geographicum

Map lichen is a crustose lichen that grows closely attached to the rocks. It looks as though someone has simply painted on the rock with a thick paint, in a combination of yellow to greenish-yellow dots on a black background. It gets its common name from its growth form. Intermingled with other lichens, it looks just like a colorful map.

The map lichen does not grow on calcareous rocks, but prefers granitic and quarzitic rocks. So, if you look for the jewel lichen, you can find limestones. And, if you look for the map lichen, you will likely find some of the harder often igneous rocks.

Map Lichen Ona naonaitok holikak taima atiktaohimayuk. Nunaoyaton mingohimayuton oyakamot. Kagiuyain avalitomit naoyokton, oyakanot mikak nipingayunahigami, ingilganitaoyuknahigami.

Naotialikiut nalongitait kanok otokaoyakhain. Canadian Rockies, ona kagiuyak taahiyukton 11 cm mik okioni 100. Kiniklogo ona kanok otokaoyahanik pijavat.

Antler Lichen
Masonhalea richardsonii

Worm Lichen
Thamnolia subuliformis sp.

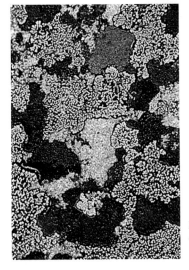

Map Lichen
Rhizocarpon geographicum

25

Sunburst Lichen
Arctoparmelia centrifuga

This rather large greenish-yellow to grey foliose lichen grows outward from a centre, developing concentric arcs (and sometimes rings) on many different rocks, but is most common on acidic rocks. As the colony ages, the inner (and older) parts of the thallus change color, and eventually drop off, leaving a clear centre portion of the colony. This may be later recolonized by the lichen, producing concentric arcs. In many sources, this lichen is placed in the genus *Parmelia*.

FERNS

Ferns and related groups are vascular plants (liquids are carried in tubes through the plant tissues, rather than transferring from cell to cell) that reproduce by spores, rather than by seeds. Some are quite small and inconspicuous. In this book, we have discussed only the most obvious ones, or those with interesting life histories.

Ferns usually have fairly large flat leaves (fronds), on a stalk. Their fronds uncurl from a "fiddlehead" in spring. They produce spores in small clusters called sori, on the underside of the leaves, or on a separate stalk.

Fragrant Shield Fern
Dryopteris fragrans

This is the most obvious fern in our area. Fronds are 15 - 20 cm. high, leathery, green above and rusty beneath. It is named for the Canadian Shield, and is common on rocky, exposed areas, usually rooting in crevices. The previous year's fronds dry out and curl about the tender base of the plant, protecting it from drying or being blasted by particles of ice in winter. The fronds remain green throughout the winter, dying back in early spring as the next year's fronds develop.

Fragrant Shield Fern Hapkoat ahigotaktoton itot. Ahigolimaitok kehimi. Atongaoyait ekiyukton napavianon kayuknagnikmi, okiomilo.

Fragile Fern
Cystopteris fragilis

A delicate fern, found on rocky slopes. When compared to the shield fern, the fragile fern is translucent, not leathery. It is also called the "bladder fern" because the sori are often covered by a hood-like cap called an indusium, which resembles a small bladder. This is hard to see, you will need to use a hand-lens.

There are a couple of other ferns in our area, use Porsild and Cody (1980) for identification.

Sunburst Lichen
Arctoparmelia centrifuga

Fragrant Shield Fern
Dryopteris fragrans / David Middleton

Fragile Fern
Cystopteris fragilis / Sam Kapolak

EQUISETACAE • HORSETAILS

Some 300 million years ago, during the Carboniferous and Devonian periods, some horsetails were huge. They grew to more than 15 meters in height, and had the diameter of a telephone pole. Most that occur today are small, less than 1/2 meter in height, but they can occur in incredible profusion. One source stated that the common horsetail is the most readily visible plant in Canada, in terms of numbers of plants.

 ## Horsetail
Equisetum arvense

This plant resembles a fern, but does not emerge with curled "fiddleheads". It has two types of stems. The fertile stems of *Equisetum arvense* are straight, unbranched, and pinkish to tan or light green, appearing in June. The spores are borne on conelike structures (strobili) at the tips of the fertile stems. The fertile stems are replaced by a dense growth of sterile green stems, 12 - 25 cm tall, with whorls of jointed side branches. In some places in our area the horsetails form a light green ground cover under willows or in protected, moist areas.

Two smaller horsetails occur along the arctic coast, *E. variegatum* and *E. scirpoides*. These lack whorled branches from the nodes, and lack an obvious central cavity. They are small (less than 12 cm), often prostrate, and frequently escape notice.

E. variegatum is most common in our area, growing on sand and clay along streams and on stabilized sandy beaches on the arctic coast. It has 5 - 10 teeth at each node, as opposed to 3 - 4 teeth per node in *E. scirpoides*.

The tissues of the horsetails contain minute grains of silica. They are often called "scouring-rushes", and were well known to the pioneers, who used them to scour pots and pans, and to polish metal or wood. Horsetails have also been used medicinally — they are strong diuretics (cause urination). They have been used as infusions to discourage head lice, and also for topical application to sores. The Inuit do not seem to use them, however. One source mentions that horsetails accumulate molecular gold (0.03 - 0.075 ppm), approximately 125 gm. per ton, wet weight (Walsh, 1986).

Horsetail Okoa atitaohimayun kinmikpaop pamioga, taima pamioton inaming. Naotiyukton hinani, alumanikmilo keyuin atani. Opingami naonaiton napavin, manikton itot kanganitok. Hapkoat naotiahanik naotigiyukton, nutak naofagaingani atongaoyak.

Horsetail *Equisetum arvense*

Equisetum variegatum

LYCOPODIACEAE · CLUB-MOSSES

Club-mosses differ from the true mosses in that they move fluids through their systems in tubes. They are larger and stiffer than the mosses, and remain green throughout the winter.

Club-Mosses
Lycopodium sp.

Two species of *Lycopodium* inhabit the arctic coast region — *L. annotinum* and *L. selago*. *L. annotinum* has spine-like tips on the leaves; it also bears spores in conelike structures at the tips of the branches, and has a creeping stem or rhizome.

L. selago is a tufted plant; it doesn't creep along the ground. Its spores are borne in small structures hidden in the axils of the leaves (at the point where the leaf branches off the plant). Its leaves are shorter than those of *L. annotinum*.

The spores of club-mosses are highly flammable — they were used in fireworks and as flash powder in the early days of portrait photography. The term "a flash in the pan" referred to the use of *Lycopodium* spores as flash powder; it was placed in a pan above the camera and ignited to produce a brilliant flash.

Club mosses Hapkoat ingilganitak (280,000,000 okioni) atongoayat. Napavin helikheyuton akhaop tomaiton. Tahetayuktotlo, sixin ski-doo nalikagiktolon.

Lycopodium annotinum

Lycopodium selago

Elymus arenarius

Grasses, Sedges, Lilies, Orchids, Water-milfoil

- Lyme-grass
  Elymus arenarius

- Bluegrass
  Poa sp.

- Arctic cotton
  Eriophorum sp.

- False asphodel
  Tofieldia sp.

- Wild chives
  Allium schoenoprasum

- Coral-root orchid
  Corallorhiza trifida

- Northern bog orchid
  Habenaria obtusata

- Mare's-tail
  Hippuris vulgaris

GRAMINAE · GRASSES · IVIK

(ALL GRASSES ARE CALLED IVIK)

The grass family is a huge one, with many species represented in our region. Identification of the grasses requires a fairly technical knowledge of the anatomy of the plant and of its flowers. We have not even attempted to deal with the grasses in this book, but have simply mentioned two species.

Grasses are wind-pollinated, and have minute and complex flower structures. A dissecting microscope and some dissection of flower parts is often necessary for identification.

Lyme-Grass, Beach-Rye Grass
Elymus arenarius

Lyme-grass, also called wild rye, is distinctive and easily recognized. It is a large, coarse grass that grows on sand dunes along the Arctic Ocean and on sandy lake shores. The leaves are blue-green; the flowers are borne in a dense, stiff spike, and the entire plant may be more than 50 cm. tall.

In many parts of the arctic, the Inuit have used the leaves of this grass to weave baskets and as an insole between the sole of the mukluk and the inner kamik.

Beach-Rye Grass Ona takiyok ivik hiugalikni hinani tagiop naoyoktok. Aoyami ihivgiotiagok kanga naotiap. Takohongoyatit naotianoit kogiktat, kakoktanik nigyaliktot itok. Naotiakhat naotikhogoyot iloani kakogo. Atongaoyait haffoma aloani kamiob atoyuktait aliolitagivlogit.

Bluegrass
Poa sp.

A fine grass that is very common along the arctic coast, and looks faintly blue when viewed from a distance. It is the same genus as the grass for which the "Bluegrass" region of Kentucky in the U.S. was named. The genus *Poa* is a large and confusing one, further complicated by the fact that it reproduces (in the arctic, at least) almost entirely by vegetative means, or by self-pollination. This means that small variations become "fixed" in a local population, making it slightly different from other populations, and thus hard to identify.

Bluegrass is a fine forage for hoofed animals such as musk oxen; it extracts calcium from the soil and makes it available to animals.

Bluegrass Hapkoat ivik koyaginak naoyukton nunami. Hapkoat ivik umingmait, tuktulo negiyuktait. Nekenagegamigik.

Lyme-grass *Elymus arenarius*

Elymus arenarius

Bluegrass *Poa* sp.

CYPERACEAE · SEDGES

The sedges are another huge group, well-represented in the arctic; there are over 100 species recorded from the N.W.T. They are easily confused with the rushes (*Juncaceae*). The stems of sedges are usually triangular in cross-section, while those of rushes are round. The following ditty may help: "Sedges have edges, and rushes are round." However, it does not always hold true; the cotton grasses, for example, are not always visibly triangular.

Sedges are usually, but not always, associated with marshy or wet areas. They vary tremendously in size. Many form tussocks, which have caused many a turned ankle. Tussock tundra covers large areas of the low arctic.

Arctic Cotton, Cottongrass, Kangoyak
Eriophorum sp.

These lovely plants have become a trademark of many arctic areas. The "heads" of these plants are strange flowers with the petals modified into white, silky strands (the "perianth bristles"). These later assist in seed dispersal by wind.

The cotton-grasses are beautiful. You don't notice them when they are not in fruit, but they form great drifts of silky white in wet areas and along the edges of tundra ponds when they are blooming and their seeds are maturing.

There are about six species of *Eriophorum* in our area. Two of these, *E. angustifolium* and *E. triste*, have several nodding terminal spikes ("heads" of "cotton") per flowering stem. The other four have a single one. One differentiates among *E. callitrix*, *E. scheuchzeri*, *E. russeolum*, and *E. vaginatum* by whether the plant forms tussocks or has stolons (low horizontal branches that can take root), and by the shape of the fruiting heads and the color of the scales at their bases. Use Porsild and Cody (1980) to identify the arctic cottons. In our area, the single-flowered species most likely to form pure drifts at the edges of lakes or tundra ponds is *E. scheuchzeri*. *E. callitrix* forms small tussocks (10 - 20 cm), and *E. vaginatum* forms large ones (20 - 40 cm), and can occur over large areas. *E. russeolum* is not quite white, but cream-colored to tawny.

In many areas, arctic cotton forms a successional stage — the tussocks begin on a wet area, or a saturated slope, and mature to create the particularly devilish surface known as tussock tundra. As the tussocks age, they support a diverse plant community of woody plants, dwarf shrubs, and moss colonies. Eventually, these crowd out the sedges, and fill in the spaces between tussocks — and the tussock tundra changes to a wet shrub tundra.

Tussock tundra is dense enough, and can become dry enough to support tundra fires; it is the only type that can do so. In some dry summers, thousands of acres smoulder for weeks on end. The ecological

Eriophorum augustifolium

Eriophorum scheuchzeri / Noreen Rodrigues

Eriophorum callitrix

37

role of fire in the maintenance of tussock tundra is interesting — fire does not kill the arctic cotton plant that forms the tussock. It removes the thatch of dead leaves, etc., and kills off many other species, such as *Rhododendron*, blueberries, willow, and dwarf birch, that have colonized the tussocks. Once this competition is removed, the tussock tundra is set back to an earlier stage of succession. It is thought (Young, 1989) that tussock tundra may be maintained in some areas by intermittent fires.

The Inuit use the flowerheads of the cottongrass as stuffing for mattresses and as tinder. They also use it as wicks for the kudlik or oil lamp. The "cotton" is arranged in a thin layer along the side of the lamp, with one end down in the seal or caribou fat. As the fat melts, it wicks up the strands of the cottongrass, and burns slowly. The woman tends the kudlik with a soapstone or wooden paddle, carefully pushing bits of fat up into the base of the flame, and keeping the "cotton" spread out thinly so it draws correctly.

Kangguyak, Kangoyak Hapkoat kangoyat atokpagait kudliup manighainut. Kangoyatayuton okiotinago. Atuktahainik okiokat. Tunoklo, nation oghoaniklo ohogiyutait. Igloina ekikahogo, atkotmon enikotoheyuktak. Oghoa unakagami ekomagiheyutok.

Nunami ioloani napavin Inupiat hapkoat nekegeyuktait. Avingan pokoyukamigin, totkotigiblogit nekehait. Inuit avingan hitaini piyuktait hapkoat. Negenagailgit taimaton, egablogitlonit.

LILIACEAE • LILY FAMILY

The lily family is a large family of usually conspicuous perennials that has been adopted as garden plants and is highly cultivated all over the world. They are monocots (members of the plant class Monocotyledonae), with parallel leaf veins and flower parts in multiples of three.

This family is represented by only a few species along the arctic coast.

False Asphodel
Tofieldia sp.

To those from the south, the false asphodels are tiny and inconspicuous, but if you look at them with a hand lens, you will be able to see their intricate beauty.

The flowers of *Tofieldia* are typical lily flowers, with flower parts arranged in threes or multiples of three. These flowers form an oblong "head" on a slender stem, or "scape." The leaves are very iris-like, flattened, and clasping each other. They emerge from the base of the plant and have the parallel veins typical of the monocots.

There are two species in our area. *Tofieldia coccinea* has reddish-purple flower heads, and a single leafy bract (specialized leaf below a flower) halfway up the stem; its leaves are more than 3 mm wide, and clasp each other like iris leaves. *T. pusilla*, is yellow-green, lacks a bract on the stem and has narrow basal leaves (less than 3 mm) which do not clasp each other.

Tofieldia pusilla

Tofieldia coccinea

Tofieldia coccinea

Tofieldia Ona ehiviotiakit naotiagit ovani atongaoyakmi. Avaleton hamani ona tainaitok naoyuktok. Angeletoamot ehiviogoni, takohongoyatik naotianoagaitok. Naotiagik mikakton Lilyton itot.

Ehivgiotiagok ona. Avaletok ona hamani naohimayok. Angelitaomot taotokoni naotiak. Atongaoyait ehimagihaotmot pehemayutot itot.

Wild Chives
Allium schoenoprasum

Wild chives are far more common in Alaska and on the western slopes of the Mackenzie Mountains than in the central arctic, but they do occur as far east as Coppermine.

Wild chives are easy to recognize — use your nose! The characteristic onion smell when you crush a leaf is a dead giveaway. Their pink-to-purplish flowers on long (1 cm) pedicels are arranged in a globular umbel. For an arctic plant, they are relatively tall, up to 10 - 40 cm.

Wild chive leaves are round in cross-section, hollow, shorter than the flowering stem, and arise from several bulbs. The bulbs look and taste like small commercial onions.

Both the leaves and the bulbs can be used in flavouring stews, salads, butter, etc., just as one would use commercial onions. They are not common enough in the central arctic to be used much by the local Inuit, but the Inupiat in Alaska use them all the time. One of the most important archaeological sites in North America is called Onion Portage after the abundant growth of wild chives along the Kobuk River in that area.

Beware of a similar species that occurs in Alaska and the western arctic, *Zygadenus elegans*, or the death camass. It is larger, and has greenish white flowers arranged in an elongated raceme, and flat leaves. Its bulbs do NOT smell like onions. This plant contains extremely poisonous alkaloid compounds that can cause death.

ORCHIDACEAE • ORCHID FAMILY

Orchids produce "irregular" flowers; they are not radially symmetrical. (Many flowers are radially symmetrical — if you cut them in half through the centre, each side will be a mirror image of the other. Irregular flowers can be cut in only one way to create two mirror image halves.)

All orchids in our area are insect-pollinated, usually by mosquitoes. Only female mosquitoes feed on blood; males never do. Both sexes feed on nectar, and are important pollinators of many arctic flowers.

Orchids produce their pollen in tiny club-shaped packets called "pollinia." These are suspended within the flower, protected from wind and rain. The insect lands on the lip of the flower, which drops slightly, opening the passage to the nectary. As the mosquito feeds, its head and thorax come into contact with the sticky pollinia. One to several detach and are carried away by the mosquito. As the mosquito feeds on another

Wild Chives *Allium schoenoprasum* / J. Irons

orchid, the pollinia may be transferred to that flower's stigma, fertilizing the ovum. Each fertilized ovum becomes an embryo, which develops into a seed.

In our area, two species of orchids occur in the Mackenzie delta, and along the coast from Coppermine to Bathurst Inlet, but not on the arctic islands.

Coral-Root Orchid
Corallorhiza trifida

This interesting little orchid contains no chlorophyll, so is not green, but a pretty pinkish brown. It is a "saprophyte", getting its nutrients from organic material in the soil. It accomplishes this through a complex relationship with soil fungi, a "mycorrhizal" relationship. Because of this interrelationship with specific soil organisms, wild orchids are almost impossible to transplant. It's best not to try; leave them in their native soil.

The whole coral-root orchid plant is yellowish brown to purplish and lacks green leaves of any kind. The flower lip is yellowish or whitish, often spotted with purple. The plant is usually from 8 to 12 cm tall when in bloom. The coral-root orchid occurs on the mainland in the arctic, and in southern Greenland, but not on the arctic islands. It usually grows in calcareous soils.

Coral-Root Orchid   Ona alangayok atongaoyak. Hongayangitok. Hongayagnia atongaoyap imaitok chlorophyll, ima iamkmik, carbonmiklo sukangotryuktok hekenikanikmi. Coral root orchid jkehemi taimailiulimaitok. Napavin iloani nunami negeyukton honavaloknik, oyuktototon.

Northern Bog Orchid
Habenaria obtusata

This robust little orchid has a single (usually) basal leaf, is usually light green, and less than 9 cm. tall. The flowers, in a terminal spike, are yellowish green. Look at them closely with a hand-lens, and you will see that they are upside down (compared with the normal position of an orchid flower). They have slender spurs that contain the nectar. Try this: insert the point of a lead pencil into the flower of one of these little orchids. The pollinia will usually spring down and stick to the lead, just as they do to the head of a mosquito (Porsild and Cody, 1980).

Like the coral-root, the northern bog orchid is really a plant of the boreal forest, and extends beyond the treeline to the coast in the Mackenzie delta, the central arctic, and on Hudson Bay, but does not reach the arctic islands.

Coral-root Orchid
Corallorhiza trifida
David Middleton

Corallorhiza trifidia

Northern Bog Orchid *Habenaria obtusata*

Northern Bog Orchid Ona atongaoyak hongayaktok, inminik nekeliuyuktok. Orchid hapkoat doanani onakinikmi naotiyukton, hamani ekiton. Bonoanik naotiyukton imaitonik pollinia. Kiktogiat polagangamikik, nekehakhiutot heknaktomik, bonaot hapkoat nipilikpatot kiktogiat niagoanot, ahinotaok atongaoyanon piplogik. Taima takhaolikpakton kogiktanoat kiktogiap niagoani.

HALORAGACEAE
WATER-MILFOIL FAMILY

Strangely enough, most members of this family are not aquatic, and occur in Australia! However, the few members of the family that occur in North America are aquatic, or grow in water with parts of the plant emerging from the water.

Mare's-Tail
Hippuris vulgaris

If you use your imagination a bit, this plant does look a bit like the tail of a horse, or, more likely, a donkey. It has a fleshy stem, often red, and whorls of simple leaves. The small flowers are borne in the axils of the upper stem leaves, in a ring around the plant, but they are not obvious. Mare's-tail usually grows in shallow ponds, 15 - 20 cm deep, but can occur in somewhat deeper water. When it does grow in deeper water, the stems become elongated, and the leaves can be as much as 6 cm in length, much more flexible and limp than those on the part of the plant above the water.

There are two species in our area, *H. vulgaris* and *H. tetraphylla*. *H. vulgaris* is most common, growing in fresh water, while *H. tetraphylla* occurs in saline or brackish water. *H. vulgaris* has 6 - 12 rather narrow leaves per whorl, and its leaves are longer than the internodes (distance from one whorl of leaves to the next). *H. tetraphylla* has 4 - 6 ovate leaves per whorl, each shorter than the internodes.

Ducks feed on mare's-tail, and wild-food enthusiasts use it as a pot-herb, or cook it in chowders, according to Janice Schofield (1989). She describes it as tasting very "green". The Inupiat and Yupik of Alaska cook it in water with seal oil and add seal blood to make a soup. The Inuit of the central arctic do not use it.

Mare's-Tail Ona naotiat naotiyokton tahiganoani, hinanilo koganoanilo. Tingmiat negeyuktait. Avunikmiut alaskami Inupiat egayoktait imakmik, natiomlo oghoanik. Elani natiom aoganik avoyoktain. Ovagot taima atoyuitavot.

Mare's Tail *Hippuris vulgaris*

Muskox feeding on willows / Joe McDonald

Trees & Shrubs

- Willows
  Salix sp.

- Net-veined willow
  Salix reticulata

- Least willow
  Salix herbacea

- Felt-leaf willow
  Salix alaxensis

- Green alder
  Alnus crispa

- Dwarf birch
  Betula glandulosa

SALICACEAE · WILLOW FAMILY

The willow family includes the poplars, aspens, and willows. The balsam poplar (*Populus balsamifera*) is the only poplar that occurs in the central arctic; some stunted groves of poplar are found in the Mackenzie delta, and near Coppermine. The aspen (*Populus tremuloides*) doesn't reach the coast, but is found inland. Aspens and poplars are trees of the boreal forest, not of the tundra.

Willows do occur in the tundra biome, but are characteristic of the plant communities of the low arctic. The number of species of willows drops off dramatically north of the arctic coast; only six species are found on Victoria Island or other arctic islands.

 ## Willows, Okpeet
Salix sp.

The willows are a vital part of the flora of the arctic coast. They are important soil stabilizers, and provide shelter and food for wildlife. Willow buds constitute the major portion of the diet of the ptarmigan; arctic hares and lemmings feed on their bark and twigs, as do musk oxen and caribou. On the mainland of the central arctic, willows are an important food of caribou. They feed on the twigs and buds of birch and willow in winter, and on the leaves and catkins in summer (Heard and Gray, in Hall's *People & Caribou in the Northwest Territories*, 1989).

At times, musk oxen in our area feed selectively on willows, wandering from patch to patch. The ox grabs a branch of willow in its mouth, and strips the leaves from it with a twist of the head and neck. This produces very characteristic feeding damage, branches stripped of leaves, with the green twigs torn away. The musk oxen on the mainland in the central arctic tend to follow the "greening" willows in the early summer, feeding low on the shores of the coast early in the season, and moving higher into the uplands as the willow foliage matures.

The Inuit have often utilized the willow. Twigs, especially those of dead plants, are used for fuel. The flexible branches were used in the construction of drying racks, drum hoops, the shafts of fish spears, and kayak ribs. Young leaves and buds are rich sources of vitamin C, and were frequently eaten, especially in the spring. The children of Bathurst Inlet say they eat the "fat of the willow". They strip away the outer bark of twigs of approximately 6 mm. diameter, then scrape off the white cambium layer with their teeth. It tastes faintly sweet.

Willow bark contains salicin (hence the genus name, *Salix*), a compound of salicylic acid, once used in the formulation of aspirin.

As spring comes to the North, one of the most obvious signs is the swelling of the willow buds. These are covered with fuzzy scales, and are the "pussy willows" of springtime. The bud scales fall away to reveal equally furry catkins, which elongate quickly, with the stamens pushing out through the "fur" of the male flowers, and the pistils, through the fur of the female flowers.

Willows *Salix*

Willows *Salix*, bud

Willows are dioecious, i.e., the staminate (male = stamens) and pistillate (female = pistils) flowers are on separate plants. The flowers (and later, seeds) are borne in catkins (dense wormlike inflorescences, which may be erect or pendulous). In many species, the flowers of both sexes (both the developing male stamens and the style and stigma of the female pistil) are bright red. The male catkins are conspicuous early in the season when they are producing yellow pollen, and the female catkins are more obvious later in the summer when they release their downy seeds. Willows are pollinated by bees, mosquitoes, and flies. They are an important source of both nectar and pollen early in the summer, when few other flowers are in bloom.

There are about 42 species of willows recorded in the N.W.T. Willows frequently hybridize, making identification difficult. If you want to identify the willows, it is best to use a local guide to the flora. For systematic keys to the willows, see Porsild and Cody (1980), Porsild (1957), Welsh (1974), and Huelten (1968).

Okpeet (All willows are Okpeet.) Ingnevikmont atoyutait. Kayaliugagamikto kelaotinonlo. Atongaoyait havaotegaloagit. Henahegagata negeyutait. Keyok hapkoat niakohuititon itot. Olugianaityaotelit. Ingilganitak ilihimayat hapkoat tamoyutak ologiaholegagamik. Alaskami Inupiat hapkoat bilgahogit ogviliuyutait.

 ## Net-Veined Willow
Salix reticulata

This very common low willow resembles the bearberry, but the leaves are much more leathery, with a waxy surface. They are also more rounded and less tapering toward the petiole. It is usually less than 4 cm tall, with erect catkins.

When the leaves emerge in the spring, they are covered with fine white hairs. These interrupt the flow of cold air across the surface of the leaf, yet permit sunlight to enter, creating a miniature greenhouse in which the sun can raise the temperature of the surface of the plant several degrees above the surrounding temperature (Savile, 1972). This allows the willow to begin photosynthesis under colder conditions than most plants. The hairs wear or fall off within a few days, as the surface of the leaf toughens and becomes waxy.

The leaves of the net-veined willow (and other willows) often bear red insect galls. These galls are composed of plant tissue — an attempt by the plant to wall off an intruder in its tissues. Open a red gall, and you will find a small caterpillar feeding on the inside of the gall. It is the larva of a moth, and will remain inside the gall until the spring, when it emerges as an adult, mates, and lays eggs in the soft tissue of the new leaves. Tiny (less than 5 mm) bright red galls on willow leaves are often formed by mites, small eight-legged arthropods related to spiders and ticks.

Salix, male

Salix, female / David Middleton

Net-veined Willow
Salix reticulata

Salix reticulata with moth galls

Least Willow
Salix herbacea

This tiny (less than 1.5 cm), creeping willow is characteristic of snowbanks where the snow stays until late in the season. Its minute catkins are often almost hidden among the leaves. The least willow flowers and produces seed very quickly, a necessity since it is exposed to the sunlight for only a portion of the summer.

This is the most northern of the willows, and it is the only willow that occurs north of the 80th parallel.

Felt-Leaf Willow
Salix alaxensis

This willow forms an erect shrub or small tree. The tops of the leaves are dull green, and the undersides and even the young twigs are covered with a velvety white mat of hairs. This furry covering is really obvious in the spring, when the long hours of sunlight and rising temperatures cause the buds to begin to swell.

The felt-leaf willow forms dense thickets, often growing to a height of 2-3 m, especially in areas protected from the wind.

BETULACEAE
BIRCH FAMILY · AVALAKIAK

(AVALAKIAK REFERS TO ALDERS AND TO THE BIRCH FAMILY.)

This family includes the birches and the alders. They are monoecious, having both staminate (male) and pistillate (female) flowers on the same plant. The staminate catkins droop, and the pistillate ones usually stand erect.

Green Alder
Alnus crispa

These shrubs or small trees reach a height of 2-3 m in protected areas. It is not common on the arctic coast, but is locally common at Bathurst Inlet. Alder is more characteristic of the boreal forest, not the tundra, but does extend its range beyond the treeline in protected areas.

The male catkins of the alder develop first, and become long and drooping, producing a powdery yellow pollen. The "cone-like" female catkins appear later, first green, then becoming dark brown. They stay on the plant throughout the winter, and provide a good identifying mark. The green alder has larger leaves than almost any other plant in the area. These shiny leaves are oval in shape, somewhat crinkled, with serrate margins.

Least Willow *Salix herbacea*

Felt-leaf Willow *Salix alaxensis*

Green Alder
Alnus crispa, male catkins

Alnus crispa, female catkins

Alders are used for firewood by the Inuit; the wood has also traditionally been utilized for construction of wooden objects like drying racks, tent poles, and kayak ribs, though not as frequently as willow. In Alaska, the Inupiat use poultices of alder leaves for insect stings and bites.

Avalakiak Hapkoat napatonoat nunami kikiktaongitomi naoyokton. Keyogiyutait inevikmot, napagiageblogelo hanalgoteliuyuktaitlo. Inupiat Alaskamiut atoyutait atongaoyait bovikagangamik, kikohigangamiklo.

 # Dwarf Birch
Betula glandulosa

On the arctic coast, this birch is almost always prostrate, seldom exceeding 30 cm. in height. It is one of the best examples of the "krummholz" growth habit. "Krummholz" is a term used for a growth form that develops because of winter-pruning of woody plants by wind-driven snow crystals (Arno and Hammerly, 1984). The plant becomes molded by pruning of all twigs sticking out of the snowdrift that develops in the lee of a rock or hummock. Many plants form krummholz, but the birches and willows provide the most obvious examples in our area.

The birch (other species of birch, like the paper birch, *Betula papyrifera*, not the dwarf birch) is an important tree to peoples of the forest. They use the wood for fuel and for building, for snowshoe frames, dogsleds, and furniture. They use the bark for containers, baby cradles, tinder, and (in the past) for canoes. The sap is boiled down to make a sweet syrup or sugar, or is used as a spring tonic or medicine for mouth sores. Leaves and buds were used as medicine, or to make tea. The Inuit traded with the Dene for rolls of birchbark to be used as tinder for starting fires, and for birch poles to use as tent poles.

The dwarf birch was probably used (by the Inuit) only for firewood. Ptarmigan feed on the buds and catkins, and small passerine birds feed avidly on insects visiting the blooming catkins. Just-unfolded birch leaves are sticky on the underside; the children (of Bathurst Inlet, at least) stick them to their ears and make "earrings" of them.

Avalakiak (See above, alders & birches.) Ona keyok atoktaoginatok, keyokagninimi. Keyogeyutait iglooliugaloahugo, hunavalunmiklo. Amit boliuhugit, nutakap lglihaniklo, egoalaotegeblogit, kayaliookpat. Amiit egablogit sukaliuyutiat, melahiliughotiklo, imaluighutiklo, havaotegiblogit kanikmot, Atongaoyait havaotegivatait, teeliukgaloahogik. Inuit himaotegeyuktait itkilinot ekighoatihan. Toatbalagamik arcticmi hunageyuitiat, keyokgenatait.

Dwarf Birch *Betula glandulosa*

Betula glandulosa

Star Chickweed *Stellaria longipes*

Bistorts, Sorrel, Pinks, Bladder Campions

- Mountain sorrel
  Oxyria digyna
- Bistort
  Polygonum viviparum
- Mouse-ear chickweeds
  Cerastium sp.
- Star chickweeds *Stellaria* sp.
- Arctic bladder-campion
  Melandrium affine
- Purple bladder-campion
  Melandrium apetalum
- Sea-beach sandwort
  Honckenya peploides
- Moss-campion
  Silene acaulis

POLYGONACEAE
BUCKWHEAT FAMILY

This large family of herbaceous (non-woody) plants is characterized by a sheath formed by thin stipules at the joints of the stems. Around the world, it includes many important food plants, such as rhubarb and buckwheat, and many plants important to waterfowl, such as the smartweeds.

Mountain Sorrel, Sweet-Leaf, Heeknakotit
Oxyria digyna

The leaves of this plant grow to a height of 5 - 7 cm; and the flower stalk grows to 30 cm. The kidney-shaped and succulent leaves are bright green in summer, changing to brilliant red in August. The flowers, only briefly present, are not as obvious as the seeds. The whole inflorescence forms a branched raceme of reddish flowers soon changing to red seeds, each surrounded by a flat, translucent wing. It grows in damp areas, hillside seeps, and swales which are not too thick with grasses. To find it, look for the reddish flower stalks.

The leaves of the sweet-leaf plant are high in vitamin C, and are very tasty, either raw or cooked with sugar for a rhubarb-like dish. There's unimaginable pleasure in finding the lush leaves of this little plant when hiking on a hot day in the arctic. Munching a handful while hiking under a heavy pack raises both your energy level and your spirits.

The mountain sorrel is circumboreal, occurring around the northern hemisphere, and has been used as a treatment or preventative for scurvy for centuries.

The Inuit use relatively few plants; this plant is undoubtedly one of the most important. It is actively sought in early summer, and is most often eaten fresh, though some people preserve the leaves in seal oil. *Oxyria* leaves also are sought by geese, musk oxen and caribou; the roots are eaten by lemmings, voles, and arctic hares.

Heeknakotit Oayami oonaktomi, omatetot itot heknakotit mamakhevagtot. Natenami nunami naoyoktot. Naonaitot napavia, aobayagami. Negeyaoginatok koyaginak.

Bistort
Polygonum viviparum

Bistort grows in thick patches, and blooms until late in the summer. Height varies, usually from 15 - 30 cm in our area.

The flowers are white, borne in a dense spike. In this family, it is impossible to distinguish the sepals from the petals; all are colored and resemble petals.

Mountain Sorrel *Oxyria digyna*

Oxyria digyna / Sam Kapolak

Oxyria digyna

Just below the flowers, a series of small bulbils develop, often sprouting while still attached to the plant. Bulbils are not seeds, but miniature bulbs that fall from the parent stalk, and are able to take root and become established during the same growing season in which they are produced. The plant reproduces mostly by vegetative means, by division of the rhizomes, or by the bulbils. Most of the flowers are sterile (occasionally the bistort does produce seeds). Leaves are dark green, shiny, and narrow.

The bistort often grows in areas of high soil fertility, near animal dens, bird nesting sites, or human habitations. The pecan-shaped rhizomes have long been used by the Inuit, and the leaves and bulbils were often eaten. The bulbils also are sought by ptarmigan and small seed-eating birds.

Bistort   Ona kakoktak naotiak napavit takokhaoyot mamatot, egablogit tiamakafoglonit. Ingilganitat kekeyutait nattiom oghoanik. Atongaoyait naoyuktot, Katagagagamik nutat naofayoktok. Akilgik, avingatlo negeyutait.

CARYOPHYLLACEAE • PINK FAMILY

A large family of widely diverse species, all with opposite leaves, flowers with (usually) 5 petals. In our area, it includes the chickweeds, mouse-eared chickweeds, sea-beach sandwort, bladder-campions, sandworts, and moss-campion.

Mouse-Ear Chickweeds
Cerastium sp.

This herbaceous plant with showy white flowers bearing five notched petals grows to a height of about 30 cm in our area. The mouse-ear chickweed is easily recognized because of the rounded tips of the petals, and its hairy leaves, which do somewhat resemble mouse ears.

This genus is frequently found in bird-nesting areas where the soil has been enriched by droppings.

Mouse-Ear Chickweed   Ehivgiotiagok ona naotiak. Mitkolik avingaob hiutatot.

Star Chickweeds
Stellaria sp.

This chickweed is also frequently found below or around bird nests. It also has white flowers, but the plant is smaller than *Cerastium*, usually less than 20 cm tall. The star chickweeds are characterized by having 5 obviously-divided petals; each petal is split in two, connected where it inserts into the calyx. The flower seems to have 10 petals. The tips of the divided petals are sharp-pointed, perhaps the source of the genus name,

Bistort *Polygonum viviparum*

Mouse-ear Chickweed *Cerastium*

Stellaria longipes / Sam Kapolak

"Stellaria" = stellate or starlike. Growing in tight masses, the chickweeds do look like galaxies of small stars dumped on the ground. The chickweeds usually reproduce vegetatively by small buds that form in the axils of the leaves, persist through the winter, and fall off dried stems in spring.

Chickweed is widely used around the world as a potherb, salad herb, flavoring, and medicinal herb. It was not traditionally used by the Inuit.

Chickweed Hapkoat kayaknakton atongaoyan, naotiyokton kobanoat anakatakvianin.

BLADDER-CAMPIONS

These are herbaceous and perennial, odd plants with an inflated calyx. There are two species, both quite distinct, in our area.

Arctic Bladder-Campion, Arctic Lychnis
Melandrium affine

The arctic bladder-campion is easily recognized, as nothing else in our area really resembles it. It has a bladder-like inflated calyx, which becomes larger as the flower matures. It can be distinguished from the other *Melandrium* in our area in that it has 5 large, notched white petals extending from the tip of the inflated calyx. There are usually 3 flowers per flower stalk, and these are erect, rather than nodding. The plant is usually 5 - 20 cm tall. *M. affine* prefers gravelly or sandy spots, and often grows near sik-sik burrows or dens of other animals.

Bladder-Campion Ona piniktok naotiak. Kakoktanoanik atongaoyalik. Boviktaton iliyuktok naohimahagangamik. Naotiahait boviktami naotiyokton igloobaknoaton, hekengob unakhimaya. Kayonagnikmilo ogkohimayuktok.

Purple Bladder-Campion, Nodding Lychnis
Melandrium apetalum

This species is also unique. Its calyx is almost globular, inflated like a little Japanese lantern, with deep purple stripes. Petals are purplish pink, and very small, usually dried up. This plant usually has a single flower per flower stalk, and that flower is definitely nodding; but straightens up as the seeds mature. The plant is usually 8 - 20 cm tall.

M. apetalum is a plant of wet areas, along streams, in moist meadows, and along lake shores. It is not too common, but seems to occur in large numbers in certain years.

Purple Bladder-Campion Ona atongaoyak boviktalik naotiakhainik naotigiyuk. Japanimi japanin atuyukton tetegamik kuliliughimayut onoahiutigiblogit. Ona atongaoyak binihakhimayuton japanin kuliutaiton, kulitun kehemi.

Arctic Bladder-campion
Melandrium affine / Sam Kapolak

Melandrium apetalum

Purple Bladder-campion
Melandrium apetalum

Sea-Beach Sandwort
Honckenya peploides

Another very odd plant, the sea-beach sandwort resembles a sedum on first glance. It is a prostrate plant which seldom exceeds 5 cm in height. It is a halophyte (literally, "salt lover"), and grows on sandy beaches exposed to salt spray, forming a compact mat with branched stems buried in the sand. Its opposite yellow-green leaves are fleshy, and may be clustered tightly together, resembling a rosette.

The sea-beach sandwort is dioecious, with male and female flowers on different plants. The flowers, which are borne at the tips of the stems, have 5 green sepals, which are more obvious than the 5 spatulate white petals. You'll notice male flowers with 7 - 10 stamens, and a small pistil, and female flowers with smaller petals, undeveloped stamens, and a large pistil. The seedpods are round and leathery, and can disperse by floating on water.

Karen Johnson (1987) reports that this plant is edible, raw or cooked, and that it has also been used as fodder for pigs and sheep. I have no indication that the Inuit people have ever used it.

Sea-Beach Sandwort Hapkoak atongaoyat okioktaktomi naoyoktok. Hiugami naoyoktot, hapkoak imakanimi. Atongaoyaini imakmik pehemayugtok. Kahakoni atongaoyain naniliyayuktok.

Moss-Campion
Silene acaulis

The classic "cushion plant" — this lovely little plant grows in the harshest of conditions in blowouts on sand dunes or eskers, or in cracks in rocks, as well as in fairly dry tundra. It develops a long tap-root which anchors the plant and can extract water and nutrients from deep in the ground.

The leaves and branches form a compact cushion. Air flows over the cushion, like the stream of air over an airplane wing. This arrangement provides considerable protection from the drying winds of winter. Snow easily covers the entire plant; no living parts are exposed. In summer, there is maximum exposed leaf surface for photosynthesis, and minimum exposure to the elements.

The flowers of the moss-campion are quite showy. They are rose to magenta in colour (with rare white variants), 1 - 1.5 cm in diameter, and extend above the cushion. They are insect-pollinated. The seeds develop in small upright 3-parted capsules on stiff stems and disperse by being blown over the snow.

Moss-Campion Ilihimayvut ona biniktok naotiak. Mitkotekaviktoton itot. Napaktonoaliktoton naoyukton nunami. Atongaoyahiat nakoyumik naotigiagani. Napagiktot napavin nunamon, oyagamilo, komnini kayunaknimi, anogikmilo hokhaongiyoiton.

Sea-beach Sandwort *Honckenya peploides*

Silene acaulis

Moss-campion *Silene acaulis*

Scurvy-grass *Cochlearia officinalis*

Mustards

- Pallas' wallflower
  Erysimum pallasii
- Yellow wallflower
  Erysimum inconspicuum
- Scurvy-grass
  Cochlearia officinalis
- Cuckoo-flower
  Cardamine pratensis
- Tansy-mustard
  Descurainia sophioides
- Smooth whitlow-grass
  Draba glabella
- Arctic bladderpod
  Lesquerella arctica

CRUCIFERAE · MUSTARD FAMILY

The mustard family contains a number of plants that have been extremely important to man throughout history. The family includes cabbage, kale, broccoli, cauliflower, turnip, radish, and others, including rapeseed, from which canola oil is extracted.

The Cruciferae is a plant family that is very easy to recognize. The four petals are arranged in a cross shape (cruciferae = crucifix = cross). There are six stamens; the four inner ones longer than the two outer ones. The seeds are borne in siliques (long, tubelike seedpods) or silicles (short, wide, flat pods) which elongate as the seeds mature.

The family may be easy to recognize, but its individual members are not! It is a large family with many representatives in the arctic. The keys in Porsild and Cody are incompletely illustrated (some show flowers, and others show only the seedpods), so one cannot fall back on it as readily as a reference. If you are interested in really working out the mustards, you will have to work from some of the scientific literature on the group, or collect two specimens, one with flowers and one with seeds, and use Porsild and Cody.

Mustard Amigaiton hapkoa atongaoyat mustanmuitan. Naonaiton hapkoak naotiahak. Hetamanik naotialgik. Huiktokagangami Inuit napavikton itonik. Atikaktok ima Cruciferae-mik talvanga napavikton. Ilovikhivikni naoyokamik.

 ## Pallas' Wallflower
Erysimum pallasii

Thank goodness, this one is easy to recognize! The pink to magenta flowers of the wallflower are large and very fragrant, in a raceme that begins flowering while the stem is so short that the whole plant appears to be a rosette of leaves. The stem elongates to about 20 cm, and the inflorescence becomes almost globular, like a huge lollipop. Smaller flower clusters that form late in the season do not elongate; but bloom at the base of the plant, among projecting siliques. The leaves are narrow, lanceolate, 5 to 7 cm in length.

Erysimum pallasii is often found near bird-nesting areas, where the soil is rich in calcium and nitrogenous compounds. It is a biennial or short-lived perennial, and flowers only once in its lifetime. In Bathurst Inlet, it often grows in close association with arctic poppies, scurvy grass, *Draba glabella*, and *Saxifraga rivularis* on limestone islands that are occupied by nesting gulls.

A similar species is *Parrya arctica*, which occurs on the arctic islands and in the east of our area, but is uncommon on the mainland. It is scentless, and the flower clusters do not form a globular raceme. The flowers may be light violet or creamy-white.

Pallas' Wallflower *Erysimum pallasii* / Sam Kapolak

Pallas' Wallflower Ona a naotiahoat, naotiagit naotiyoktok nunamibloni. Ulamiktanik naotiagayukton, nugolakton itoni nunami. Takonaton kobanoat oblokaviani.

Yellow Wallflower
Erysimum inconspicuum

The only other wallflower in our area is a tall yellow wallflower that grows on sandy banks, and on river terraces. *E. inconspicuum* is far from inconspicuous. It can be up to 50 cm tall, and is an attractive light yellow. The 4-petalled flowers are 14 - 18 mm in diameter, blooming in a ring around the elongating raceme. The flowers begin blooming at the base of the raceme, and the inflorescence elongates as bloom progresses toward the tip. At the same time, the developing curved siliques protrude from the withering petals, elongating to 3 - 5 cm. The plant may consist of a single flowering stalk, or several flowering branches. Leaves are simple, lanceolate, with weakly toothed margins.

The yellow wallflower is really a plant of the boreal forest, but extends beyond the treeline in the central arctic, reaching the coast at Bathurst Inlet, in the Mackenzie delta, and on the north slope of Alaska.

Scurvy-Grass, Spoonwort
Cochlearia officinalis

The scurvy-grass is not a grass at all, but clearly in the Cruciferae. A halophytic (adapted to growth in salty soil) and nitrophilous ("nitrogen-loving", thriving in soils rich in nitrogen compounds) plant, *Cochlearia* often grows near traditional nesting sites of seabirds or under raptor nests near the edge of the sea. It is a biennial, forming a non-blooming rosette the first year, and blooming the second.

The flowers are white, on light-green, leafy stems that often lie almost flat on the ground. The basal leaves are rounded, arrowhead-shaped, or kidney-shaped, with slender petioles. They are fleshy ("succulent"), an adaptation to conserve water within the tissues of the plant, and do look like little spoons, hence the common name, "spoonwort".

The leaves are high in vitamin C, but not particularly tasty. The early sailors and explorers who overwintered in the arctic suffered from scurvy, caused by a lack of vitamin C in their diets; they sought the scurvy-grass as a dietary supplement. They even baled it (with poor results), and made a "tincture" of it (scurvy-grass ale) by soaking it in vinegar or alcohol (Schofield, 1989). However, a number of plants were called "scurvy-grass", so this name in an early journal does not necessarily refer to this particular species.

Yellow Wallflower
Erysimum inconspicuum

Scurvy-grass *Cochlearia officinalis* / Sam Kapolak

Scurvy-Grass Ona atoktaovaktok ingilgani Kabloonat akoikakataktoni. Ayoikhimangitot inuyamingni nunami ingilganitaktot, nigiyokhotik kablunat nikainik hikolaniklo. Nikit hapkoa nikaotianginamik anialakivaktot, kigotaikhotiglo tokogaloakhotiglo. Nalvaktait hapkoa naotiat nakoyot nigiyami aniaknaitomik.

Cuckoo-Flower, Bitter Cress
Cardamine pratensis

This large mustard has white-to-pale-lavender flowers up to 2 cm in diameter in a terminal raceme that may be somewhat flat-topped. The pinnate stem leaves have 5 - 10 leaflets, and the basal leaves are quite variable, but usually contain several leaflets, more rounded than those of the stem leaves. The name "cuckoo-flower" comes from these basal leaves — they are so variable the plant is considered "crazy" or "cuckoo".

Cuckoo-flower is one of the largest, most obvious mustards in our area. It grows in moist marshy areas, often along the sea coast, and is very obvious among the slender stems of the marsh grasses when it is in bloom. Although this plant does produce siliques which elongate from the centre of the flowers, it reproduces mainly from leaf-buds on the basal leaves (Schofield, 1989). The terminal part of the leaf is capable of rooting if it touches the ground.

There is another *Cardamine* in our area, *Cardamine digitata*. It has white flowers, and is similar to *C. pratensis*, but slightly smaller; it rarely exceeds 15 cm here. The inflorescence of *C. digitata* forms an oval, while that of *C. pratensis* is shaped like a flattened umbrella. The stem leaves of *C. digitata* are like fingers of a hand, hence "digitata", while those of *C. pratensis* are almost fernlike. Unlike *C. pratensis*, *C. digitata* doesn't grow in marshes, but in the hummocky tundra, or near bird nest sites.

Tansy-Mustard
Descurainia sophioides

This mustard has small yellow flowers, clustered tightly together when first blooming, and elongating as the bloom moves down the raceme. The developing siliques project from the centre of the flowers, causing the flowers to appear spiky. The stem leaves are finely dissected; they resemble fern leaves. The basal leaves are present at first but wither as the bloom progresses.

This is a common plant in the western part of the central arctic. It blooms in late June at Cambridge Bay and Holman, and is often abundant in areas where the soil has been disturbed, such as around settlements, along roads, and in dumps. There is a lot of variation in the height of the plant in different parts of its range; at Bathurst Inlet, it grows to a height of 1.5 m; at Holman, to about .5 m.

Cuckoo-flower *Cardamine pratensis*

Cardamine digitalis

Tansy-mustard *Descurainia sophioides* / Pat Thagard

73

Smooth Whitlow-Grass
Draba glabella

Draba glabella has white flowers, borne on single or forking stems, 10 - 20 cm in height. In the early stages of its bloom, the petals are closed. Later, the flower opens out, the cross shape of the petals can be distinguished, and it changes appearance dramatically. Smooth whitlow-grass has distinct basal leaves that are spatulate, with a few teeth, about 1 - 5 cm. long; they are covered with soft hairs. The stem leaves are slightly smaller, also weakly-toothed.

The relatively short, flat seed pods are hairless, with a stem (pedicel) as long as the silicle. As the seeds mature, the pod "dehisces", or opens, the sides fall away, and the seeds drop. Eventually only the margin is left, a little ghost of the pod, resisting the winds of late summer.

Draba glabella grows in lush stands near rich sources of animal dung, especially on bird islands or below nesting cliffs.

Arctic Bladderpod
Lesquerella arctica

This low, tufted little mustard arises from a stout taproot, and has a basal rosette of greyish green spatulate leaves, many of which are slightly cupped, and have a single blunt tooth on each side. The leaves are covered by unusual silvery stellate hairs (several hairs arising from a single spot on the leaf, diverging to form a star), easily visible with a hand lens. The yellow flowers are borne in loose racemes at the end of several widely-diverging (5 - 20 cm) flower stalks. The siliques (seedpods) are globular, resembling tiny balls, each with the dried remains of the style at the tip, hence the common name of "bladderpod".

The arctic bladderpod is a plant of the stony barrens, gravel ridges, or sandy areas. It has a circumpolar distribution, but is more common in the North American arctic, where it occurs across the arctic coast from Alaska to the north coast of Greenland. It is common on the southern coast of Banks and Victoria Islands, at Cambridge Bay, on King William Island, and on the Boothia Peninsula.

Smooth Wiltlow-grass
Draba glabella

Arctic Bladderpod
Lesquerella arctica / Noreen Rodrigues

Potentilla nivea / Sam Kapolak

Buttercups, Poppies, Rose family

- Richardson's anemone
  Anemone richardsonii
- Few-flowered anemone
  Anemone parviflora
- Marsh-marigold
  Caltha palustris
- Yellow water crowfoot
  Ranunculus gmelinii
- Birdfoot buttercup
  Ranunculus pedatifidus
- Pygmy buttercup
  Ranunculus pygmaeus
- Arctic poppy
  Papaver radicatum
- Mountain avens
  Dryas integrifolia
- Seaside potentilla
  Potentilla egedii
- Shrubby cinquefoil
  Potentilla fruticosa
- Snow cinquefoil
  Potentilla nivea
- Marsh five-finger
  Potentilla palustris
- Cloudberry
  Rubus chamaemorus

RANUNCULACEAE
BUTTERCUP FAMILY

The Ranunculaceae is large and varied family. Without using a key, it is difficult to concisely describe family characteristics; see Porsild & Cody (1980) for a key. In all the members of the Ranunculaceae in our area, there are many stamens and pistils, crowded together into a globular or ovoid head. Locally, this family includes the anemones, buttercups, and marsh-marigolds. The monkshoods, larkspurs, and columbines also belong to this family, and occur in the North, but do not occur in our area.

All members of this family are poisonous, although the poisonous factor in marsh-marigold is rendered harmless by cooking. The old saying, "There are no poisonous plants in the Arctic." is simply NOT TRUE.

WINDFLOWERS · ANEMONES

The anemones are called "windflowers" because they are generally alpine flowers, often growing in windy places, and are tall enough to be blown about by the wind.

Many of the arctic anemones are "snowbank" species; they occur at the edges of deep, late-melting snowbanks. Contrary to what one would think, the plants that occur at the edges of snowbanks are not necessarily the most hardy plants, nor those with the greatest "arctic affinities" (Young, 1989). Snowbanks become established during the soft, heavy snows of autumn, and become deepest where the most snow collects over time. This means that the plants under that snow are the ones receiving the greatest insulation and protection from the dessicating winds of winter. They also benefit from a steady source of reliable moisture during the growing season. Snowbank species are "quick starters"; they are able to get going very quickly when exposed by snowmelt.

In the anemones, petals are not present, but the sepals are colored and resemble petals. The anemones in our area all have a whorl of leaves surrounding the flowering stem below the inflorescence.

Anemone Hapkoat atihimayun anogim atongaoyait. Anogikanikmi naotiyokamik. Nunaptini hapkoat naotiyukton apotiganikmi aoyami naotiyukton apotailihakninmi.

Richardson's Anemone
Anemone richardsonii

This showy anemone is named for John Richardson who was the surgeon-naturalist with the Franklin expedition of 1819 - 22. In the Richardson's anemone, the sepals are bright yellow, with pointed tips. It is the only northern anemone with yellow flowers. The basal leaves are divided into 5 parts, and the stem leaves into 3 parts. The stem leaves are sessile, and arranged in a whorl about halfway up the stem. The plant is usually less than 20 cm high, with one flower per flower stalk.

Richardson's Anemone *Anemone richardsonii*

Anemone richardsonii

Richardson's anemone can be found in bloom until late in the season by searching in areas where snowbanks persist. It also grows in moist sheltered areas and under willows.

Richardson's Anemone Kogetak naotiak, apotikanikmi naoyoktunlo. Keneahialogo napavin ketkani ona atongaoyak, atongaoyalik.

Northern White Anemone, Few-Flowered Anemone
Anemone parviflora

A delicate white anemone, usually less than 20 cm tall, with one flower per flowering stalk. The backs of the 5 blunt sepals are silky and tinged with blue. The 2 - 3 sessile stem leaves are each divided into 3 lobes, and are arranged in a whorl around the stem. The basal leaves are dark green, glossy, and divided into 3 - 5 bluntly-toothed lobes.

In the arctic coast region, this anemone commonly occurs at the edges of high tundra ponds, and in protected areas where snowbanks linger into the summer. It seems to prefer calcareous soils. It can be confused with the flower of the akpik, or cloudberry — but the akpik has both petals and sepals, and its stem leaves are alternate rather than whorled, and much larger than the stem leaves of the anemone. In full bloom, the anemone is much taller than the cloudberry, and much more flexible.

Marsh-Marigold
Caltha palustris

The northern marsh-marigold is unlike the robust marsh-marigold of the south, though this is the same species! It is delicate for a marsh-marigold, but sturdy for a tundra plant. Marsh-marigold grows in or at the edges of tundra streams, roots often completely submerged. There are no petals, and the 5 sepals are bright yellow, rounded, less than 2 cm in diameter.

The leaves are heart- or kidney-shaped, with a glossy surface. The plant is often "decumbent", lying in and flowing with the water, but the flower stalks bend up and emerge from the water. When it is erect, the whole plant is usually less than 20 cm tall. "Caltha" means "cup", and refers to the shape of the flowers.

This plant occurs all over the northern hemisphere, and got its name in the Middle Ages, when it was called "the flower of the Virgin Mary", or "Mary's gold", and "marybuds". In various parts of the world, the marsh marigold is known as an edible herb, though it is toxic when eaten raw. It must be dried or boiled in two changes of water in order to remove the poisonous glucoside (protoanemonin)(Schofield, 1989). Eating it is not recommended, and it is not used by any of the peoples of the North.

Marsh-Marigold Ona naotiak naotiyoktok imakanikmi. Napavinlonit imakmi naoyokton. Kogetanaonik atongaoyalik. Atongaoyait ulamiktan. Umingmaop tomaiton itot.

Northern White Anemone
Anemone parviflora

Anemone parviflora

Marsh-marigold *Caltha palustris*/Sam Kapolak

Koyaginak nunami naotiyokton. Atihimayut ingliganit imaton hapkoat atongaoyat Virgin Mary.

BUTTERCUPS

The buttercups can be confused with many other arctic plants, including the anemones, the marsh-marigold, some saxifrages, and the potentillas, but usually can be distinguished from all the others in that they have a peculiar waxy shine to the petals and sepals — they look like they are coated with plastic. Buttercups have colored petals and sepals, and the stamens and pistils are numerous, grouped together into a globose or ovoid head, which becomes very obvious when the petals fall off.

The name "buttercup" comes from the shape of the flower, and an old English children's ditty. Parents used to touch the flower to their children's chins, saying, "Let's see if you like butter!" If it left a golden powder, the child was supposed to like butter. This golden powder, of course, was pollen.

Several high-arctic buttercups occur only (in our area) in the King William Island/Boothia Peninsula and Pelly Bay area. In those locations, check *R. hyperboreus*, *R. sabinei*, and *R. sulphureus*.

We will illustrate only a few of the buttercups here, and refer the reader to Porsild and Cody (1980) for keys and more complete descriptions of the buttercups of the continental Northwest Territories.

Buttercups Hapkoa naotiat mikitkiat allanit naotianit, kakoktatkialo. Atia "buttercup" nutakat makpiganginit pihikmayok. Angayokan kahaktiyoktait nutakan taploani okalaotiplugit ima "Patamik mamagioknakhiotin". Kogitanikpat taploa patamik mamagiyokhaot. Kogiktanoak naotiakhak.

 ## Yellow Water Crowfoot
Ranunculus gmelinii

Ranunculus gmelinii is an amphibious buttercup; it grows with its roots in standing water or in the shallows of small streams. It can be submerged or stranded by changes in water level, and will survive. It is not commonly found, but where it does occur it can be extremely numerous, often covering the surface of the water with a carpet of yellow flowers. It produces long stolons, which root at the nodes, producing new plants.

The leaves of this species are important in identification. They are small (1.5 cm or less), and divided into three to five divisions, each of which is deeply divided again. It can be distinguished from the truly aquatic buttercups (*R. aquatilis* ssp.) by the fact that its leaves are more robust — those of the aquatic buttercups look like small down feathers.

Yellow Water Crowfoot *Ranunculus gmelinii*

Ranunculus gmelinii

Birdfoot Buttercup
Ranunculus pedatifidus

This buttercup grows from a tufted base rather than creeping stolons, to a height of 10 - 30 cm. The flowers are showy, pale to bright yellow, with rounded petals. Sepals are also yellow, only slightly smaller than the petals. The basal leaves are kidney-shaped in outline, and are deeply divided into 5 - 9 narrow lobes. The stem leaves are sessile, divided into 1 - 3 narrow lobes, almost appearing to be several separate leaves.

A plant of calcareous soils, this buttercup grows on moist gravel, sand, or grassy areas. It is pollinated almost entirely by flies (Willard and Zwinger, 1972), and has little odor. The term *pedatifidus* means "bird-footed", and the leaves do look like the tracks of cranes.

Pygmy Buttercup
Ranunculus pygmaeus

The pygmy buttercup is tiny, often no more than 3 cm high, so small that an entire plant could be contained in your cupped hand. It grows at the moist edge of snowbanks that persist long into the summer, often in association with the dwarf arctic willow (*Salix herbacea*) and mountain sorrel (*Oxyria digyna*).

The pygmy buttercup has one flower per stem, and basal leaves with long petioles. The leaves are roughly three-lobed, although some of the lobes are deeply cut.

This buttercup is more common on the arctic islands than on the coast.

PAPAVERACEAE • POPPY FAMILY

This is a widespread family of plants that has become highly cultivated the world over, because they are large, brightly colored, and grow well in a wide variety of conditions.

Opium (from which the painkilling drug, morphine, is derived) is commercially extracted from the sap of the seed capsule of poppies cultivated for this purpose in the Middle East.

Arctic Poppy
Papaver radicatum

Poppies are true solar collectors — their flowers are shaped to collect and reflect the rays of the sun onto the ovaries in the center of the flower, raising the temperature just enough to encourage rapid maturation of the seeds. The flower head rotates to face the sun, keeping the rays constantly focused.

Birdfoot Buttercup
Ranunculus pedatifidus

Pygmy Buttercup
Ranunculus pygmaeus

Arctic Poppy
Papaver radicatum / Sam Kapolak

P. radicatum is approximately 12 - 20 cm tall, with a single large pale yellow (almost greenish-yellow) flower on a slender scape. Several scapes arise from a tuft of sparsely-hairy basal leaves which are roughly lance-shaped, but divided pinnately into 3 - 5 lobes. Hundreds of minute seeds are borne in an ovoid capsule which is nodding at first, but becomes erect as it matures.

Take a look at the maturing flower capsule. Notice the dark hairs on the outside of the capsule. These absorb the heat of the sun, and help raise the temperature of the capsule a couple of degrees over the surrounding air, speeding maturation of the seeds. The tiny black seeds ripen in the capsule and are dispersed through holes in the top as the stalk is shaken by the wind.

The poppy group is genetically extremely complex, and involves plants with several different chromosome numbers, so there is a lot of variation and they are difficult to identify. There are 3 - 4 species of poppy which are characteristic of our area. The most common is *P. radicatum*, described above. *P. hultenii* is taller (25 - 30 cm), with the petiole of the leaves about five times as long as the blade, it occurs in the western part of the Canadian arctic and around the Coppermine area. *P. keelei* has dark green leaves, hairless on top, divided into 5 parts, with lateral lobes quite narrow. It occurs along the arctic coast west of the Mackenzie, and on the NW coast of Banks Island. To the east, *P. cornwallisensis* occurs on King William Island and on the Boothia Peninsula; it is a dwarf plant, less than 12 cm, with pale yellow, white to pinkish yellow flowers. (See Porsild and Cody, 1980, for key characters.)

P. radicatum and *P. hultenii* are both species of gravelly, well-drained soils, while *P. keelei* prefers moist herbmats, and *P. cornwallisensis* occurs in calcareous gravelly soil that is rather wet.

Arctic Poppy Hapkoa kogetanoat naotiat hekenikmik beyukton. Atongaoyait ogvinoaton iliyukton hekenikmik kitka piplogo onaktiplogit naotiahat iloani naotikton. Ona naotiat hakatahoni hekenikmot beyuktok.

ROSACEAE • ROSE FAMILY

The rose family is an important family throughout the world. Such food plants as the apple, crab apples, blackberries, raspberries, strawberries, pears, plums, and cherries are all in the rose family. Popular garden flowers such as the cinquefoils, hawthornes, flowering crabapples, burnets, and, of course, the rose, are in this family.

Most plants in the Rosaceae have five distinct sepals and five petals. They have numerous stamens, and one to many pistils. Many are shrubs, or at least have a woody base.

Papaver hultenii / J. Irons

Mountain Avens
Dryas integrifolia

The mountain avens is the official "flower of the Northwest Territories". It is a good choice, for these creamy white flowers sometimes dot the tundra as far as the eye can see. The mountain avens is a woody plant, and forms low mats. The leaves are dark green on top, and the undersides are covered with white, woolly hairs. The specific epithet "integrifolia" refers to the leaf margins; they are relatively smooth (entire), with only a few scallop-shaped teeth on the lower half.

The flowers of the mountain avens are stunning. There is a single flower (about 2.5 cm in diameter) per plant, borne on a hairy stem; the whole plant is about 4 - 12 cm tall. As in the poppies, the inflorescence acts as a solar collector. Its parabolic shape focuses the rays of the sun on the developing ovaries, and the whole inflorescence rotates to face the sun.

As the seeds mature, the styles of the pistils elongate tremendously, and become plumose (featherlike). At first, they twist together, but as the inflorescence matures and dries, the styles untwist and spread out, opening to catch the winds as the seeds loosen from their base. At times, in late August, the air seems filled with snow — seeds of the *Dryas* being transported on the wind.

Dryas is a calcium indicator, growing on calcareous soil. It forms thick mats on gravelly, well-drained soil in areas scoured by steady winds in winter. This low mat growth habit allows the snow to collect and the dessicating winds to pass over without pruning it. Because the mats are quite tightly intergrown, the mountain avens is an excellent soil stabilizer. It has a fibrous mat of roots that grips the soil. Its woody branches and leaf petioles capture the dirt, dust, and dead leaves, building up a thick humus layer beneath the mat. In addition, through the utilization of nitrogen-fixing bacteria in nodules on its roots, *Dryas* enriches the soil with nitrogen compounds (Willard and Zwinger, 1972).

Mountain Avens Nunatiami naotiagogiyaoyok ona. Kakoktan naotiagit hekenikmik beyukton. Hakatahotik hekenikmon, atongaoyait ekegatahotik ketla nalaotikatahogit hekenikmon.

CINQUEFOILS

The cinquefoils are a large genus, worldwide, containing a number of species very popular for northern gardens because they are cold-hardy perennials.

When flowering, they are fairly large plants, mostly due to their ascending flower stalks. Some are woody, and most are partially woody, at least at the base. The flowers are all five-petaled; most local ones are yellow.

Seven to nine species of *Potentilla* occur in our area. Because of space limitations, we've described only a few of them. See Porsild & Cody (1980) for keys, and range maps.

Mountain Avens *Dryas integrifolia*

Dryas, seedhead

Dryas integrifolia, mat

Seaside Potentilla
Potentilla egedii

In this small, prostrate cinquefoil, the characteristic long, smooth, arching runners extend from a central flowering rosette. These runners (often red) root freely, producing new plants. Flowers are yellow, seldom more than 7 cm high. The leaves are pinnately compound, glossy green, with grey to white undersides.

P. egedii is a true halophyte, seldom growing beyond the sea spray zone. It carpets the ground in places; many other plants cannot tolerate high salt levels, so competition is reduced. However, when it does grow beyond the spray zone, it does not look like the same plant! It is tall, to 24 cm, with large shiny leaves that stand up rather than lying flat, and larger flowers than in sea shore specimens. I have found it growing away from the spray zone in only one place, however, by a freshwater marsh on an island in Bathurst Inlet, some 90 m from the sea. There are no seaside colonies of this species on that particular island at this time, however. *P. egedii* has a very limited distribution north of the arctic coast.

Known as Pacific silverweed along the Pacific coast, *P. egedii* has long been highly valued by the peoples of the coast; patches of the herb were owned only by chiefs, and the roots were used both as medicine and food. The Inuit of the central arctic do not seem to use this plant, probably partially because it is not very common, and is quite small in their area.

Seaside Potentilla Hapkoat atongaoyat naotiyokton tagiop hinani, tahivalonilo. Tagiop hinanitot mikatanoat, halaplotik nunami naotiyokton, tahivaloniton angiliyokton hikhikton eghevayuton. Mikanoat atongaoyat napavikmik hanianongahiyukoton, nunamon totgangata nutak naovatok. Hapkoat koyaginak nutami hirani naotiyokton, hiugakanikmi tagiomi.

Shrubby Cinquefoil
Potentilla fruticosa

These are small woody shrubs (usually less than 50 cm in our area) with reddish-brown shredding bark. Flowers are bright yellow, 2-3 cm in diameter. The palmately-compound leaves have short petioles or are sessile; the 3-5 leaflets are narrow and quite silky on both sides.

P. fruticosa has a wide distribution, from high meadows and muskeg south of the treeline to the tundra, but does not extend beyond the coast. It is the only woody (shrublike) *Potentilla* in our area, thus easy to recognize. According to Karen Johnson (1987), the cinquefoils are high in tannins, and have been used in the tanning industry, and for antiseptics, astringents, and tonics. The Inuit do not use this plant except for fuel.

Shrubby Cinquefoil Ona atongaoyak angiyunik kogiktanik naotialik. Tahiyukton hekonon tekiploni, pinihiyuktok naotiagangamik.

Seaside Potentilla *Potentilla egedii*

Potentilla fruticosa / Sam Kapolak

Shrubby Cinquefoil *Potentilla fruticosa*

Daonanikmuiton pinikotegiyuktiat iglooni helatani, helamilonit. Balamiot imaton tiayuktat "cinquefoil" "tallimat algiat." Tallimanik naotiagagamit. Naotiat okoat tallimanit pikagamik algatot.

Snow Cinquefoil
Potentilla nivea

This bright yellow *Potentilla* is loosely-tufted, with branched flowering stems about 20 - 30 cm high. Most of the leaves are basal, palmately compound, with three leaflets. These are dark green above, dull white underneath, and are deeply-toothed.

This species is common, and tends to prefer sunny sites and rocky calcareous soil. It is particularly common near bird nesting areas and animal dens. Several sources mention that the leaves are high in Vitamin C, but there is no indication that the Inuit people used it.

In our area, *Potentilla nivea* can be confused with *Potentilla rubricaulis*, both are about the same size and color yellow. In *P. nivea*, the basal leaves have three leaflets (are 3-parted), while in *P. rubricaulis*, they usually have five (are 5-parted).

Marsh Five-Finger, Marsh Cinquefoil
Potentilla palustris

The common name of this plant comes from the leaves — they are quite large, have a reddish tinge, and are palmately compound, with five leaflets, hence "five-finger". The stems are quite red, and may be upright (15 - 25 cm) or decumbent (lying on the ground). The flowers are dark reddish-purple, with sepals longer than the petals, and curved up around the central disk. They resemble dark strawberries set upright on starry disks.

P. palustris occurs in wet areas, sometimes growing in the water. It is also quite salt-tolerant, and grows along the coast, in beach-grass communities, and sometimes in association with *P. egedii*. It is a late-bloomer in our area, mid-July to early August. Karen Johnson mentions that the Siberian Inuit dried the leaves to make a tea, but the people of the central Canadian arctic do not use it.

Marsh Five-Finger Ona naotiak takiyuk naotiyoktok imakanikmi tahevaloni. Itinikmi imakmi naotiyoktok. Naotiagik aobayakloktok, aogtot banikhimayuton itot.

Other Potentillas Amigiaton alaketaton imaiton atongaoyat nunaptini. Tamaita kogiktat, naonahivaktot kitoyahain. Amigiaton naotiyokton oblunkavini, hitinilo, inektoklikavinilo, nuna atuktaohimayok nakohivakgmi timailigangami.

Snow Cinquefoil *Potentilla nivea*

Potentilla nivea (prob.)

Marsh Cinquefoil
Potentilla palustris

Potentilla palustris

Cloudberry,
Baked-Apple Berry, Akpik
Rubus chamaemorus

This attractive low (5 - 8 cm) plant is dioecious; male and female flowers are produced on separate plants. In the single white flower, either stamens or pistils are functional, but not both. Each plant bears 1 - 3 leaves; these are leathery and 5-lobed, with sawtoothed margins, somewhat resembling maple leaves.

The fruit of this plant is highly regarded by Inuit and Kablunak alike. It resembles a raspberry, is red when immature, and passes through a series of different colours, from salmon to amber, to pale yellow when it is ripe. It is a soft and juicy fruit, and has a rich flavor not unlike baked apples. The fruits ripen in early August in our area.

The akpik plants grow in moist places, usually where there are many mosses — the plants tend to be scattered out over the tundra. In the arctic, almost everyone seeks these berries avidly. Most are eaten fresh, but the Inuit occasionally preserve them in seal oil or make jam.

Akpik Nalonaiton hapkoa atongaoyat. Kakoktanoat naotiat mamakhotiklo baongat. Naotilihagangamik aobayatot. Naotiagangamik aolaisigalit. Atongaoyait hapkoat ajikotagiyait takoyapta pinikota. Akiliyuton aogangamik. Elipkagangamik hogaogiyukton. Alaskamuit Inupiat avoyuktait baongak, akpitlo alatlo atongaoyait. Totkoyuktait aihaotikavikmon.

Cloudberry *Rubus chamaemorus*

Rubus chamaemorus

Saxifraga tricuspidata

Saxifrages

- Grass-of-Parnassus
  Parnassia palustris
- Golden saxifrage
  Chrysosplenium tetrandrum
- Bulblet saxifrage
  Saxifraga cernua
- Alpine saxifrage
  Saxifraga nivalis
- Heart-leaved saxifrage
  Saxifraga punctata
- Prickly saxifrage
  Saxifraga tricuspidata
- Purple mountain saxifrage
  Saxifraga oppositifolia
- Brook saxifrage
  Saxifraga rivularis
- Yellow marsh saxifrage
  Saxifraga hirculus
- Yellow mountain saxifrage
  Saxifraga aizoides

SAXIFRAGACEAE • SAXIFRAGE FAMILY

This family has a lot of representatives in alpine and arctic areas around the world. Most sources state that the name "saxifrage" is derived from the Latin *saxum* (a rock) and *frango* (to break) (Coombes, 1985), and evidently it comes from the fact that the saxifrages often grow in the crevices of rocks, appearing to break them apart. However, in his excellent *Colorado Flora: Western Slope* (1987), William Weber disagrees. He cites Gerard's *Herbal*, of 1633, as stating: "This name, *Saxifraga*, or Saxifrage, hath of late been imposed on sundry plants farre different in the shapes, places of growing, and temperature, but all agreeing in this one facultie of expelling or driving the stone out of the Kidneies, though not all by one meane or manner of operation." Weber does go on to say that the saxifrages have been far more important as garden plants than as sources of drugs, however. Take your pick.

The saxifrages are quite variable, but most that occur in the North have basal leaves which are often leathery or succulent and flowers borne at the top of a long (for the size of the plant) scape (flowering stem). The flowers typically have 2 styles (divisions of the pistil), which may be as obvious as the petals. Three genera occur in our area. *Parnassia* and *Chrysosplenium* are easy to recognize, and the rest of the saxifrages are in the genus *Saxifraga*. We have added a systematic key to help with the identification of species in the genus *Saxifraga*, as it is well represented in the arctic.

 ## Grass-of-Parnassus
Parnassia palustris

This lovely plant is *not* a grass, but a member of the saxifrage family. It's an example of the way common names can lead one astray! The large white flowers (1.5 - 2 cm in diameter) on 15 - 20 cm stems are surrounded by heart-shaped basal leaves on long petioles. *P. palustris* has a single small clasping leaf less than halfway up the flowering stem; its petals are longer than the sepals. A similar species, *P. kotzebuei* (also found in our area) usually lacks the clasping leaf, and has petals shorter than the sepals.

Some authors (Weber, 1987) now place the grass-of-Parnassus in a separate family, the Parnassiaceae, because it has 4 styles fused into one pistil. Using a hand lens, take a close look at the flowers of this plant. The 5 normal stamens alternate with 5 odd sterile staminodia, each bearing a fringe of yellow glands.

Grass-of-Parnassus is one of the latest plants to flower in the brief arctic summer; it begins blooming in late July. It occurs in wet areas, along the edges of streams, by the edges of tundra ponds, or along the seashore. It often blooms so thickly that one can imagine that the name "grass" came from the profusion of stems. It is named for Mt. Parnassus, in Greece.

Grass-of-Parnassus *Parnassia palustris*

Grass-of-Parnassus Ona naolikpaktok okiakmi. Kayoknanimi naoyoktok koyaginak nunani. Atiktaohimaploni imaton Mt Parnassus-mit Greece-mit, Mediterranean tagiogata hinani.

Golden Saxifrage, Northern Water Carpet
Chrysosplenium tetrandrum

This is an odd little plant that doesn't really look like a saxifrage. It is low, usually less than 4 cm tall in our area, with 4 yellow-green sepals and no petals. The small, lobed, succulent leaves form a scalloped collar just below the flowers. When ripe, the ovary splits open to reveal the seeds, like golden bronze eggs in a miniature nest. There are several fleshy basal leaves, each with three to seven lobes.

The golden saxifrage is a plant of moist stream edges, hillside seeps, and shady banks. It is also commonly found around old campsites, near old meat caches, or around denning sites, as it does well in moist soil enriched by animal droppings. A lush growth of this plant spangles the soil around the ancient antler dwellings at the Nadlok ("Crossing Place") archaeological site on the Burnside River, an Inuit camp occupied from the 1400s to the 1700s.

SAXIFRAGES

Most plants in the genus *Saxifraga* have a stiff central scape bearing the flowers, and distinct basal leaves. The seed capsules form at the apex of the scape, and have constricted apical pores, which limits the number of seeds that can be shaken out at a time.

This genus is a good example of an adaptation to winter dispersal of seeds, which is made far more effective by the fact that sea and lake ice forms effective bridges, and drifting snow levels out the ground. Add the high winds of winter, and we find that dispersal of seeds, bulbils, and plant parts is relatively easy. The stiff, upright scape of the saxifrages releases seeds a few at a time, when it whips back and forth in the wind. This means that some of the seeds are not released until snow and ice cover has been established, making long distance dispersal far more likely (Porsild, 1951).

Saxifraga is a complex genus which is an important one in the arctic, in terms of numbers of different, recognizable species. The differences between species, once you get into it, are distinct, and identification does not require a specialized vocabulary (such as that needed for the grasses, or the willows). It is interesting and fun to see how many different saxifrages you can find in an area.

Saxifrages Hapkoa naotiat nunami koyaginak naoyokton. Atia ona saxifrage ima naonaiktaohimayok "Oyakanik ahigoktigot." Oyakani naotiyokton.

Golden Saxifrage *Chrysosplenium tetrandrum*

KEY TO THE SAXIFRAGES

To assist you, we have appended a systematic key to the saxifrages. To use it, start at the first couplet, and read both choices. One will fit best, so go to the number indicated by that choice. Eventually, you will obtain an answer. Not all are covered in the species accounts, but are included to reduce confusion engendered by coming to an insoluble couplet in the key.

1. Plant a compact mat, foliage much reduced, leaves opposite, on prostrate stems; flowers large (1 - 1.5 cm), bluish-purple to magenta, on short pedicels above the matted foliage. . . . .
. . . . **Purple Mountain Saxifrage,** *S. oppositifolia*

   Plant not a compact mat, leaves alternate or in basal tufts, flowering stems erect; flowers white, creamy, or yellow, or, in one species, greenish purple 2

2. Flowers yellow. 3

   Flowers white, creamy, or greenish-purple 4

3. Flowers yellow, with random orange dots on petals, several flowers per stalk; foliage fleshy, light translucent green, linear leaves with small bristles on margins . . . . **Yellow Mountain Saxifrage,** *S. azoides*

   Flowers yellow, with orange dots in rows on petals, thicker toward centre of flower, single flower per stalk; leaves not as above . . . .
. . . . **Yellow Marsh Saxifrage,** *S. hirculus*

4. Flowering stem lacking leaves 5

   Flowering stem bearing leaves. 8

5. Basal leaves kidney-shaped, with distinct petiole longer than leaf itself; flowering stem hairy . . . . **Heart-Leaved Saxifrage,** *S. punctata*

   Basal leaves not kidney-shaped, petiole not distinct from blade of leaf; flowering stem smooth. 6

6. Basal leaves purple beneath; flowers in a tight panicle; two large capsules (3-4 mm) diverging in centre of flower; sepals purple, only slightly shorter than the petals. . . . . **Alpine Saxifrage,** *S. nivalis*

   Basal leaves green beneath; flowers other than above. 7

7. Flowers in a loosely branched panicle, often with only one normal flower (which is white) at the apex, others replaced by bulblets which begin to leaf out while still on the plant; leaves scalloped on tips, tapering to base, petiole not readily visible. (This sp. is not covered in the species accounts.) .... *S. foliolosa*

Flowers greenish purple, in small dense clusters on a spikelike raceme on a stout scape; no bulblets; leaves all basal, oblong-lanceolate, base tapering to short petiole, 3 - 5 cm, with rounded-serrate margins. (This sp. is not covered in the species accounts, occurs in Boothia area only.) .... *S. hieracifolia*

8. Leaves mostly basal, without distinct petioles; leaves strap-shaped, each terminating in 3 sharp points ... **Prickly Saxifrage,** *S. tricuspidata*

Basal leaves with distinct petioles; leaves lobed, varying in shape, but lacking the 3 sharp points 9

9. Stem leaves lobed, with petioles; basal leaves generally round in shape, with lobed margins 10

Stem leaves generally not lobed, usually straplike, small; basal leaves with 3 finger-like lobes, small, in a tight basal cluster; a complex group with a lot of variations, number of flowers on stem varies from 1-3 (This species is not included in species accounts) .... *S. caespitosa*

10. Single large white flower at apex of scape; reddish bulbils in axils of leaves along scape; loose colonies with erect stems widely separated from each other .... **Bulblet Saxifrage,** *S. cernua*

Often several flowers per scape; lacks bulbils; growing in compact colonies, with scapes close together .... **Brook Saxifrage,** *S. rivularis*

Bulblet Saxifrage, Nodding Saxifrage
Saxifraga cernua

The bulblet saxifrage is a delicate-looking little plant that occurs in a wide range of habitats, from dry rocky slopes to shady areas, in small caves, or under overhangs. It is easily recognized by the red bulblets in the axils of upper stem leaves; these leaves are much reduced, almost vestigial. The height varies greatly, from 8 - 25 cm. A single white flower tops a slender scape, and the basal and lower stem leaves are kidney-shaped and divided into 5 - 7 pointed lobes. Most also have a cluster of white bulblets at the base of the stem, amidst the basal leaves.

Like the bistort, this plant reproduces vegetatively, via the bulblets, and never reproduces by seed.

Saxifraga cernua is common around settlements on Victoria Island, especially Cambridge Bay, where it spangles lush fields of dwarf fireweed and mouse-ear chickweed. It is less common on the mainland.

Bulblet Saxifrage Ona piniktok kakoktak naotianoak naovaktok Keelinikmioni (Victoria Islandmi), naokatikakhoni allanik, aopayavyaktonik naotianik, naotiakhait katagayokton naoffagiangani.

Alpine Saxifrage, Snow Saxifrage
Saxifraga nivalis

This is a robust saxifrage, often growing to a height of 20 cm. White petals contrast sharply with the reddish-purple sepals, and the developing follicles (fruits) which are also reddish. The basal leaves are leathery, shiny dark green on top and reddish-purple underneath, oval blades with serrated tips, each tapering to a broad petiole. No other saxifrage has leaves that are purple beneath.

The snow saxifrage usually grows on well-drained, rocky ledges, often among lichens. This saxifrage tends to occur as widely scattered individual plants rather than in groups. The specific name "nivalis" comes from the Latin *nivea*, which means "snow".

Two similar species occur in the central arctic. *S. hieracifolia* is more common in Alaska, the Yukon and on the Boothia Peninsula. It has similar leaves, with more distinct petioles, and greenish-purple flowers on a stout scape. The seeds are borne in purplish-black follicles. *S. foliolosa* is more delicate, with leaves shaped like those of the snow saxifrage, but smaller, with the serrations limited to the terminal 1/4 of the leaf. The flowers form in a loose raceme with (usually) only 1 - 2 obvious flowers at the apex of the cluster, or on the largest side branches. The side branches bear bulblets, which begin to produce leaves while still on the plant.

Snow Saxifrage Ona naotiak naovaktok hitokani apotikaknini, imakakninilu. Kakoktalo aopayaktolo naotiangit kalikokhaton iton. Atani atongaoya kinigokni piniktok purple-mik atavilik.

Bulblet Saxifrage
Saxifraga cernua / Sam Kapolak

Alpine Saxifrage *Saxifraga nivalis*

Heart-Leaved Saxifrage
Saxifraga punctata

On first impression, *S. punctata* resembles *S. nivalis* in size and general flower appearance. The white or purplish flowers are borne on a slender 15 - 25 cm stem which is sparsely covered with fine hairs. The leaves are quite distinctive — underneath, they are green, not purple; the blade is roughly kidney-shaped with 9 - 14 teeth and is borne on a long, slender petiole.

This saxifrage grows in moist areas, especially on mossy hillsides, and in the spray zone of waterfalls; these were photographed beside Wilberforce Falls.

Prickly Saxifrage, Three-Toothed Saxifrage, Kakilahan
Saxifraga tricuspidata

The prickly saxifrage is one of the most common saxifrages in the arctic coast region, often flowering in great drifts that color the landscape. White flowers are spotted with orange and borne on slender, fairly stiff stems, 7 - 15 cm. This saxifrage can be identified from the basal leaves alone — these are narrow (about 4 mm wide), with three distinct, sharp teeth, hence the specific epithet, "tricuspidata". There are very few "prickly" plants in the arctic — this one truly is prickly! The leaves turn bright red in fall, lending a ruddy hue to the landscape.

A very successful colonizer, *S. tricuspidata* seems to prefer dry, rocky or gravelly places, and becomes established in simple cracks in the rocks. It grows in abundance on dry algal limestone or sandstone islands in Bathurst Inlet. When the saxifrage is in bloom, the whole island appears to be frosted.

Kakilahan Hapkoat ikiton naovakton kakilahanakton. Atongaoyait pingahonik ipiktonik pilgit. Naonaitok ona naotiak naoyoktok oyagavaliani, oblokanini kikiktani kehemi, naoyoktonlo oyagakanimi, allanit naotiat naokatigiblogit. Atongaoyait aopayaktongokpaton okiami.

Heart-leaf Saxifrage
Saxifraga punctata

Saxifraga tricuspidata

Prickly Saxifrage
Saxifraga tricuspidata / Joe McDonald

Purple Mountain Saxifrage, French-Knot Moss
Saxifraga oppositifolia

This is the earliest flower to bloom in our area, beginning in June, as soon as the snow melts from its ridge-top habitats. By July, it can be found in flower only on shady, north-facing cliff faces, where the snow has persisted into mid-summer. It's an odd plant, growing successfully in habitats with the most extreme micro-climates — places that suffer the cold, dessicating winds of winter, and the baking summer sun. It grows on the high arctic islands, and southward into the Rockies at high elevations.

The purple saxifrage is odd-looking, too. It's a low, matted plant with very short grey-green overlapping leaves in four rows. Usually, this plant extends no more than 2 cm above the surface, although the bluish-purple flowers double its height. The flowers are large for the size of the plant, 1 - 1.5 cm across, readily visible to their insect pollinators.

Take a look at a plant with a hand lens; each leaf is fringed with minute rigid hairs. This is another plant that takes advantage of the snow for protection from wind dessication — the fringing hairs help hold snow about the plant until a tiny snowbank can form.

It demonstrates the typical form of an insect-pollinated mat plant — keeping a low profile through the winter, and then bursting forth with exuberant, colorful bloom in the summer when pollinators are present.

Purple Mountain Saxifrage Ona naotiak naotkayoktok naotianit allanit. Naotiliyoktok June-mi apotaiyaligangami. Anogikaknimi naoyoktok. Ihivgiogiakmiok ona naotiak — ivalokhaop kilikninoangiatotan itok. Kablunaton atia "French knot moss," naosiap kilikniaton.

Brook Saxifrage
Saxifraga rivularis

This small (3 - 6 cm) saxifrage is found in wet places, along brooks, in wet gravels at the base of cliffs, and (most abundantly) in moist areas near bird nests, or around old camps. It grows in thick stands in association with scurvy-grass (*Cochlearia officinalis*), star chickweed, and *Draba glabella* on bird-nesting limestone islands in Bathurst Inlet. The brook saxifrage ranges all across the arctic coast, on many of the arctic islands, and on the coasts of Greenland and Hudson's Bay north of the treeline. It tends to be limited to coastal areas and river drainages.

The brook saxifrage has light green stems covered with soft hairs and smooth kidney-shaped basal leaves with 3 - 5 lobes and long petioles. Each stem bears 1 to 5 small white flowers with petals about twice the length of the sepals. The overall impression of the plant is a fresh light green.

Brook Saxifrage Ona naotiak naoyoktok kobanoagiaknimi kikiktani, obloini naoyat. Naokatigiyoktait scurvy grass (ivit), naonaitot tallimanik naotiakagamik hitamaongitonik.

Purple Mountain Saxifrage
Saxifraga oppositifolia / Sam Kapolak

Saxifraga oppositifolia
Sam Kapolak

Brook Saxifrage
Saxifraga rivularis

Yellow Marsh Saxifrage
Saxifraga hirculus

This yellow saxifrage (5 - 18 cm tall) grows in clumps in wet areas, often in association with sedges, seaside arrowgrass, arctic cotton, and the purple bladder-campion.

Each plant bears a single bright yellow flower, which starts out nodding, and becomes erect as it matures. Toward the centre of each flower, the petals of the yellow marsh saxifrage are speckled with orange spots in rows, possibly serving as a nectar guide to assist insects in locating the centre of the flower.

There are no distinctly basal leaves, and the stem leaves are strap-like and sessile (with no petiole). They are often held up, quite close to the scape. In our area, *S. hirculus* can be confused with *S. aizoides. S. aizoides* has fleshy leaves somewhat clustered toward the base of the stem, and may have more than one flower per scape, while *S. hirculus* has thinner leaves, and usually has only one flower.

Yellow Marsh Saxifrage Ona kogiktak naotiak naoyoktok ivikaknimi, naopluni opingami. Ihivgiotiagok ona naotiak - takoniaktatin aopayavyaktonoit.

Yellow Mountain Saxifrage
Saxifraga aizoides

A small yellow-flowered saxifrage that grows in loose mats or clumps on moist clay and gravel, stream banks or slopes. It is usually about 10 cm tall with orange-dotted petals. The leaves of this little saxifrage are short (less than 1.5 cm), linear, and fleshy. On *S. azoides*, the petals are narrower than those of *S. hirculus*, and are dotted with orange spots at the outer half of the petal, while the spots of *S. hirculus* are located toward the base of each petal.

Yellow Marsh Saxifrage
Saxifraga hirculus

Saxifraga hirculus

Yellow Mountain Saxifrage
Saxifraga aizoides

Summer scene, Coppermine / J. Irons

Legumes or Peas

- Arctic lupine
  Lupinus arcticus

- Richardson's milk-vetch
  Astragalus richardsonii

- Alpine milk-vetch
  Astragalus alpinus

- Beach-pea
  Lathyrus japonicus

- Liquorice-root
  Hedysarum alpinum

- Northern sweet vetch
  Hedysarum mackenzeii

- Yellow oxytrope
  Oxytropis maydelliana

- Arctic oxytrope
  Oxytropis arctica

- Oxytropis arctobia

LEGUMINOSAE · PEA FAMILY

The legumes are important food plants the world over, producing food for man as well as his domestic animals. It is a common family in the arctic; there are many species, covering large areas of tundra. In flower, most legumes are colorful and highly visible.

Legumes are also "nitrogen-fixers". Through bacteria in nodules on their roots, the legumes extract nitrogen from water and add it to the soil. The flowers are "irregular"; they show bilateral, rather than radial symmetry.

It is not easy to recognize legumes by looking for characters that identify the genus. It is almost easier to recognize the species, and remember its genus.

We have omitted many of the legumes; see Porsild & Cody (1980) for systematic keys to the legumes. Their keys work best if you have access to both flowers and pods.

Pea family, Leguminosae Okaot naotiat elagiaktot amigaitotik nunaptingni elangit naonakhotik — ajikkiikaloakhotik. Naotiat hivitoyot emakmit hilamot ekayogamik, nunamotlo. Ekayoktikagamik mikalannoak omayonik. Naotiat ekayotikaktot omayoni; naopkaivakhotik naotianik alani. Kengotikagovit ekayutit omayot naotianot takoniaktotit.

Arctic Lupine
Lupinus arcticus

One of the most colorful and well-known plants of the arctic, the lupine is a large plant, sometimes reaching 25 - 40 cm. Its blue-and-white flowers in showy racemes often create a blue haze over large patches of moist tundra, late June through mid-July. The leaves are palmately compound, with long petioles; they are smooth above, covered with soft, downy hairs (pubescent) beneath. The seedpods are 2 - 4 cm long, covered with silky hairs. Occasional white-flowered "morphs" (morphological forms) are found in our area.

This plant is poisonous; the seeds especially so. They should never be sampled, even though they resemble peas. During a rain, the leaves capture a drop of water in their centres — a patch of lupines then looks like a field of diamonds in the sun!

Arctic Lupine Ona naotiat ilihimayaoliktok. Koyaginak amigaiyokton hongayalakiplotin nunami julaingogangat. Naotian hapkoat ketka nipalokangak imakangamik pinikotilikton ilivakton. Hapkoat naotiat lupine tokonaknakton, naotiahaitlo. Negetailivaklogit.

Arctic Lupine *Lupinus arcticus* / Sam Kapolak

Lupinus arcticus

Lupinus arcticus

Richardson's Milk-Vetch
Astragalus richardsonii

This species superficially resembles the alpine milk-vetch, but the flowers are much more bicoloured. In bud, they look quite pinkish, with touches of black — the calyx of each flower is densely covered with black hairs. As the flowers expand, they become whiter, but still touched with pink. The seeds are borne in reddish translucent bladderlike legumes, which lack hairs, and are quite pretty when backlit by the sun.

A. richardsonii grows in much the same habitat as does *A. alpinus* in the central arctic, mostly on well-drained sandy or gravelly soil. At Bathurst Inlet, it is common on gravel beaches, growing above the sea-spray mark. The plants that inhabit these beaches typically develop a low, prostrate growth form, with the flowering stems lying flat, often radiating from the central stem of the plant. In more protected spots, the flowering stems are erect.

Named for John Richardson, surgeon-naturalist to the Franklin expedition, the Richardson's milk-vetch is found nowhere else in the world, other than on the central arctic coast and on the western islands of the arctic archipelago (Houston, 1984).

Alpine Milk-Vetch, Alpine Crazyweed, Mountain Locoweed
Astragalus alpinus

The flowers of the alpine milk-vetch are light blue, sometimes so pale as to be almost white. They are sometimes streaked with fine purplish-blue lines, and the tip and keel of the corolla are often a darker blue than the rest of the flower. The flowers are clustered together in rather tight racemes. The leaves are pinnately compound, with 15 - 23 elliptical leaflets covered with white hairs on the bottom, and sparsely haired on top. Seeds are produced in hanging brown pods which are covered with black hairs.

The alpine milk-vetch is very common on the central arctic coast and on Victoria and Banks Islands, blooming in profusion in moist sandy or gravelly soil. In open areas it is quite prostrate, but in more sheltered areas, the stems are more upright.

The term "locoweed" or "crazyweed" is often used for species in this genus, for a couple of reasons. According to Christine Heller's *Wild Edible and Poisonous Plants of Alaska* (1985), when growing on soil rich in selenium, some members of the genus *Astragalus* take up the element, concentrating it in the plant tissues. When these plants are eaten by grazing animals, it can cause neurological disturbances, the "blind staggers". Some members of the genus also contain locoine, which causes grazing animals to "go loco", a neurological disorder in which the animal loses muscular control, moves with an irregular, shambling gait, and suffers a loss of appetite, weight loss, and eventually death. There is no direct evidence that the vetches in the central arctic produce these effects, but they should certainly not be eaten.

Richardson's milk-vetch *Astragalus richardsonii*

Astralagus richardsonii

Alpine Milk-vetch
Astragalus alpinus

Beach-Pea
Lathyrus japonicus

The beach-pea usually has pale bluish flowers, but the color may vary toward purple; they are often darker at the base. The foliage is very tender and light green, almost clammy-feeling. It is the only legume in our area with tendrils. The flowers closely resemble those of the domestic sweet pea, so much that one would expect to see this plant draped over a garden trellis.

This lovely plant has a scattered distribution in our area, occurring at Bathurst Inlet and in the Mackenzie delta. It occurs on sand dunes or in sandy areas along the seashore or at river mouths, seeming to respond more to sandy soil than to the presence or absence of salt water, although it is certainly salt-tolerant. It creeps loosely over the ground, and seldom exceeds 15 cm in height.

The young peas and pods of the beach-pea are quite tasty, almost like snow-peas. However, when used as a sole source of food (such as might occur in times of famine), they can cause paralysis (Schofield, 1989). Eat them as a snack only.

Beach-Pea Hapkoat naotiat piniktok alatkiktakton. Kakoktaogaloahotik, hongayatongoyukton. Henakton niamayami. Baongaton iloani naotiyokton. Negeyami mamaton taimanginak, egablogitlonit. Ona nekaotihaogitok, neketoagogimak. Negenalikak ona naotiat mihinaihongoyuk inuhit. Ogtokafogok mikangmik. Negenagioglogo. Ona naotiat naotiyokton tagiop hinani.

Liquorice-Root, Bear Root, Eskimo Potato, Mahok
Hedysarum alpinum

This common legume is easily recognized by its unscented pink flowers in slender racemes up to 50 cm tall, with 10 - 20 flowers per inflorescence. The bright green leaves are pinnately-compound, with 9 - 13 leaflets. The net-veined seed pods are flat, with 3 - 5 oval "locules", each with a single seed. The plant forms branching clumps. When the seeds and leaflets fall, the characteristic straw-colored Y-shaped flowering stalks remain.

The Inuit utilize the thick root of this plant, digging it out with special tools made from caribou antler. They peel off the outer covering, and eat it raw, boiled, or roasted. They claim it is best in the fall or in the spring, and look for the Y-shaped stalks when searching for the plant. It does not taste like liquorice, but does taste a bit sweet. The *H. alpinum* roots are a real favorite of grizzly bears — a bear will dig up literally hundreds of square feet of plants to feed on the roots.

This plant can be easily confused with the following plant, *H. mackenzeii*, which is poisonous.

Mahok Ona aobayangajitok naotiat negeyaoyuktok Akhanin. Inuitla nakoyut nekaotait. Akhat algahogit helikton negeyuktait. Inuitlo hapkoat mahuin negeyuktait. Mahakangak, opingamilonit mahotayukton.

Beach-pea
Lathyrus japonicus / Sam Kapolak

Lathyrus, seed pods

Liquorice-root *Hedysarum alpinum.*

Hedysarum alpinum, seed pods

Amiyakhogik negeyuktait, egablogitlonit. Mahuit hapkoat ajikotalgit tokonaknatonik atongaoyanik. Ilihimavajavat kitoli mahuktaktan. Naotiagik mahuin tipiaton, aobayangajitot.

Northern Sweet Vetch, Wild Sweet Pea
Hedysarum mackenzeii

This is a striking plant, with brilliantly colored flowers that seem almost luminescent in the long sunlight of a summer evening.

The flowers of *H. mackenzeii*, as compared to those of *H. alpinum*, are magenta rather than pink, and are definitely sweet-smelling. The flowers are larger than those of the liquorice-root, 2.5 - 3 cm long in *H. mackenzeii*, compared to 1.75 - 2 cm in *H. alpinum*. The leaves in *H. mackenzeii* are pinnately compound, similar to those of *H. alpinum*, but have silvery hairs on the undersides of the leaflets. The sections ("locules") of the seed pod are transversely-veined, rather than being net-veined as are those of *H. alpinum*.

H. mackenzeii was described by John Richardson, surgeon-naturalist with the Franklin expedition, and is reported to be quite poisonous, but all reports of its toxicity seem to trace to sources in the journals of the Franklin expedition. Its family includes the very poisonous locoweeds; so don't take a chance on this plant being non-toxic. One never sees signs that bears have been digging the roots of this plant.

Wild Sweet Pea Naotiagik hapkoat naotiaganit mahuit alangayot. Tipainlo henakton. Akhan algayuitan hamna naotiat. Tokonaknaktohaoyuk. Negetailivaklogo.

Yellow Oxytrope, Maydell's Oxytrope
Oxytropis maydelliana

The oxytropes are legumes in which the flowers are arranged in a rather compact "headlike" structure, borne on a leafless stem (scape). They have pinnately-compound leaves arising from a stout tap-root.

There are a couple of yellow oxytropes in our area, *O. maydelliana* and *O. hyperborea*. To distinguish between the two, look for papery "stipules" at the leaf bases — those of *O. maydelliana* are chestnut brown, and those of *O. hyperborea* are white or yellow.

In the arctic coast region, *O. hyperborea* occurs mostly in the west, from the Mackenzie delta to Coppermine to Arctic Sound and the west coast of Victoria Island; *O. maydelliana* is far more widespread, across all of the coast, from the Bering Straits to Baffin Island. The oxytropes (as well as many members of the genus *Astragalus*) are also called "locoweeds" because of their effect on many grazing animals. These plants contain locoine, a chemical which causes loss of muscular control, staggering, and eventual collapse and death (Heller, 1985).

Northern Sweet Vetch *Hedysarum mackenzeii*

Hedysarum mackenzeii

Yellow Oxytrope *Oxytropis maydelliana*

Arctic Oxytrope
Oxytropis arctica

The flowers of the arctic oxytrope are bright pink to magenta or deep blueish purple, and quite showy. The arctic oxytrope is similar to *O. arctobia* in that in both the flowers are marked with a broad white blaze on the "standard", the upper petal of the flower. This probably functions as an insect "guide" to assist bumblebees (the main pollinator) in landing on the lower lip of the flower. The flowers are sweetly scented.

O. arctica can be distinguished from *O. arctobia* in that its leaflets are smooth and relatively free from hairs on the upper surfaces, while those of *O. arctobia* are covered with silvery hairs. *O. arctica* is a taller plant, also, and the flowers are borne on stems longer than 8 cm., unlike *O. arctobia*. Both can be quite blue in color.

The arctic oxytrope grows in great abundance in the central arctic, but is endemic (limited) to arctic North America.

Oxytropis arctobia

The flowers of this low plant are a quite striking pink, magenta, blue or bluish-purple in colour, often with a lighter blaze on the front of the standard (upper petal). On the mainland they tend to be pink, and, on Victoria Island, a bluish purple. Only one or two to a flowering stalk; they contrast sharply with the ashy-grey foliage. The scapes are quite short, so the flowers are borne quite close to the foliage.

O. arctobia forms attractive dense cushions of velvety leaves; each leaf is pinnately-compound, and only 1.5 - 2 cm long. The seedpods mature to a dark brown or black color and are quite inflated. Without the flowers or seedpods, the foliage of this plant blends perfectly with the ground.

This beautiful little plant occurs on dry, windswept gravel ridges, where winter conditions are truly severe. It is an "endemic" plant, found *only* in our arctic coast region, occurring nowhere else in the world. It is so easily overlooked when it is not flowering that many people miss it.

Large mats of both *Oxytropis arctica* and *O. arctobia* combine with yellow oxytrope, mountain avens, buttercups, chickweed, and alpine crazyweed to create an incredible oriental carpet of color on the rocky land around Cambridge Bay and Holman in mid-July.

Arctic Oxytrope *Oxytropis arctica*

Oxytropis arctobia / Pat Thagard

Oxytropis arctobia

Autumn, Coppermine / J. Irons

Heaths and the Berries

- Crowberry
  Empetrum nigrum
- Soapberry
  Shepherdia canadensis
- Bog rosemary
  Andromeda polifolia
- White arctic heather
  Cassiope tetragona
- Bearberry
  Arctostaphylos sp.
- Labrador tea
  Ledum decumbens
- Lapland rosebay
  Rhododendron lapponicum
- Blueberry
  Vaccinium uliginosum
- Lingonberry
  Vaccinium vitis-idaea
- Alpine azalea
  Loiseleuria procumbens

EMPETRACEAE • CROWBERRY FAMILY

This family of low, sometimes prostrate shrubs is circumpolar in distribution, but has only one representative in our area. This is the crowberry, an important food plant for the Inuit.

  ### Crowberry, Blackberry, Baongak
Empetrum nigrum

Crowberry often forms a low matted ground cover over large areas, especially where there is sandy, acid soil. It is a plant of the low arctic, occurring mostly on the mainland, and is rarely found on the arctic islands.

The crowberry is an evergreen shrub, resembling miniature fir branches, but is not a conifer at all. The short fleshy leaves are so narrow they look almost tubular, and are about 5 mm in length.

Crowberry flowers are seldom noticed because it flowers when the leaves are still brown, very early in the season. Look for the flowers on plants at the edges of snowbanks. It is a real thrill to find the flowers of this plant, because they appear so briefly. Male and female flowers are both bright red, but are on separate plants. They are tiny, and nestled in the axils of the upper leaves. The male flowers are a brilliant scarlet, with long stamens protruding, capped with bright scarlet anthers. Female flowers are also red, but not quite so bright, and lack the protruding anthers.

The crowberry fruits are black berries, shiny and abundant, containing four large seeds. Crowberries are eaten fresh in great quantities by the Inuit, and were preserved in seal oil by some groups. Their flavor improves after the first frosts, and they persist on the branches all winter. They are an important food of geese, especially the snow geese. Gulls feed on them, especially during early and late summer.

Baongak Hapkoat baongak atongaoyani naoyokton Inuitnait negeyuktait. Aogangata okiahami negeyuktait. Nunami ahini natiom oghoanik avoblogik ilipkayuktait okiomi nekehait. Nunaptini opingami negeyuktakot. Apotaigangat.

ELAEGNACEAE • OLEASTER FAMILY

A family of shrubs and small trees, including both the Russian olive and the autumn olive, which have been introduced into the Great Plains areas, and now are causing concerns as escaped alien plants. Peculiar stellate hairs and scales speckle both leaves and fruits of this family, giving the undersides of the leaves a metallic sheen, and spangling the fruit with golden specks. The fruits of plants in this family are high in vitamin C (Weber, 1987).

Crowberry *Empetrum nigrum*, flower

Empetrum nigrum, fruit / David Middleton

Empetrum nigrum, fruit

Soapberry, Soopolallie
Shepherdia canadensis

This attractive shrub is quite large compared to the rest of the berry-bearing shrubs on the arctic coast, it can reach 90 - 100 cm in height. The leaves are dark green and quite leathery, and leaves, twigs and fruit are all dotted with the hairs and scales mentioned above. The undersides of the leaves are covered with shiny brown scales, producing a metallic golden sheen, which intensifies in the spring. The flowers develop very early, and are small and yellowish. The soapberry is dioecious, with flowers of different sexes borne on separate plants.

The soapberry is common south of the treeline, and in the Mackenzie delta, but is relatively uncommon along the coast. It does not occur on the arctic islands.

The bright orange-red fruits are lovely to look at, but taste quite astringent, almost like turpentine. Bears love them, however, and many groups of native peoples across the North do use them in various ways. In Alaska, the berries are beaten to a froth (like soap), and sweetened with sugar to make a dessert or a refreshing drink (Heller, 1985, and Schofield, 1989). Schofield also mentions that the whipped berries can be used as a soap. The Inuit of the central arctic do not use them, however, probably because they are uncommon in their land.

Soopolallie Imaitot piniktok aopayangajitot - aolaisigalingoyukamiklo baongak. Keyonoani naoyokton. Pinikhongoyut mamaitok kehemi. Heknaktoton mamaiton. Tipilgik mingotitot. Atikhimayun imaton ikmiut baongak. Kaogagangata ikmiutiton iliyukamik.

Koyaginak Inuit atoyutait hapkoat baongan. Nekaotigiblogit, havaotigiblogitlo. Okayuktait nakoyut tepekagangamik. Ilangik Inuit atoyuitat hapkoat baongan. Atongaoyat hapkoak naoyokton keyokanikmi. Ahinitaot naoloayuitok.

ERICACEAE • HEATH FAMILY

This family is an important one in almost every mountain region in the world, and in the the arctic as well. Almost all the woody plants on the arctic islands are heaths, and the family provides edible fruits which are important to many herbivores, some carnivores, and to Man.

According to William Weber, in his excellent *Colorado Flora, Western Slope* (1987), heath flowers are "beautiful creations, like porcelain easter-eggs into which one peers to see exotic scenes, and exotic they are, for the stamens have anthers that open by terminal pores and are often adorned with peculiar horns." Get a hand lens, and take a look!

Soapberry *Shepherdia canadensis* / Sam Kapolak

Bog Rosemary
Andromeda polifolia

The bog rosemary is a low (seldom exceeding 6 cm in our area) evergreen shrub with narrow, deeply-grooved leaves, which have the edges rolled under, and are whitish beneath.

Its nodding urn-shaped pink flowers are borne in small terminal clusters, each flower on an arched pink pedicel. They have five petals joined to make the bell, and five darker pink sepals.

These tiny urns with their openings facing downward are an adaptation to the short summers and harsh climate of the arctic. Sunlight penetrates the pinkish tissue of the urn, and warms the air within. Since warm air rises, it in turn warms the ovaries, raising the temperature of those tissues just a bit above the ambient air temperature outside the plant. The warm air stays in the miniature "greenhouse" of the urn, and is rewarmed by the sun.

As the fruits form, the capsules become erect. A darker pinkish-red than the flowers, they look like tiny apples sitting on pedestals.

Sometimes carpeting the ground, bog rosemary grows in wet tundra from the muskeg to the arctic coast, but does not occur on the arctic islands. Several authors report that it is poisonous, containing a toxin (andromedotoxin) that lowers blood pressure and causes breathing difficulties and intestinal distress (Johnson, 1987, and Schoenfield, 1989).

Bog Rosemary Piniktot ona atongaoyak, naotialik aobayavyaktonik mokpanoaton napavaini. Atilik ogvikmit kabloonaton, naotiavinoaton itot. Aobayavyanit hanigait naotiap, hekenikmot pekatata, aototikatahogo iloa. Ataninami angmanikagamit, onaknik kolvaktiyoktok, ahinongaoyuitok onaknik, iloanikafoktok. Aotomayoktait naotiahat naotiton iloani. Naonagiyokton.

White Arctic Heather,
Arctic Bell Heather, Eghotik
Cassiope tetragona

The tiny white bells of the arctic heather form a striking contrast with the dark green foliage of this low shrub. The faintly-scented bell-shaped flowers are nodding at the end of long, arching pedicels. The leaves are short and almost scale-like, appressed close to the branches. The specific epithet *tetragona* means "4-sided." *Tetra* = "four"; *gon* = "side" (as in pentagon, hexagon, etc.). When crushed, the foliage is aromatic.

The arctic heather is a relatively early bloomer, flowering along with the rhododendron. A hillside of arctic heather is truly unforgettable in full bloom. It can be confused with nothing else!

At the end of the season, many plants of the arctic heather produce oddly-shaped light yellowish-green leaves at the ends of the branches. This may be a modification to utilize lower levels of light as the days shorten.

Bog Rosemary *Andromeda polifolia*

Andromeda polifolia

White Arctic Heather
Cassiope tetragona
Sam Kapolak

The foliage of the heather is high in oils, and burns easily even when green. It was used as fuel by the Inuit when travelling on the land, and is still an important fuel in the Holman area.

Eghotik   Ona atongaoyak piniktok, hongayaktomit atongaoyalik, ulomaloktot naotiagik kakoktat. Ekoalataktot kelamik. Keyogiyuktiat nunaptini.

Bearberry, Kablak
Arctostaphylos sp.

Both black (*Arctostaphylos alpina*) and red (*A. rubra*) bearberries are common throughout our area. They form mats extending over large areas, sometimes mixed with blueberry and cranberry. Their leaves can easily be confused with the leaves of the reticulated willow, but can be distinguished by touch. The leaves of the willow are much more leathery and rounded; those of the bearberry are thinner, more flexible, and the base tapers to the petiole. The flowers of the bearberry are seldom noticed; they form in early spring (June, in our area), amongst the withered leaves of the previous year. They are greenish-white, urn-shaped, and nodding.

Bearberry leaves become a vibrant scarlet in late August and early September, coloring large areas of tundra. Those of the red bearberry are shed in the fall, while the leaves of the black bearberry remain on the plant until late in the winter. When not in fruit, the two species are difficult to distinguish; some authors consider them to be a single species rather than two. In fruit, of course, there is no doubt.

Bearberries are consumed by many birds and mammals, including bears. Their taste is rather mealy and insipid, but the Inuit enjoy and use them, frequently mixing them with blueberries and crowberries.

Kablak   Hapkoat ilihimayakot atongaoyat. Aopajalakotiyuktok okiami, pinikhitiyoktot tavongagalok. Nunaptini malgoyuk imaiton, aopayakton, kinagiktotlo. Tamaita hapkoat atoktaoyuktot nunaptini.

Bearberry *Arctostaphylos alpina*

Arctostaphylos alpina

Arctostaphylos rubra

Arctostaphylos, fall color

Labrador Tea
Ledum decumbens

The Labrador tea is (in our area) a low shrub with narrow, alternate evergreen leaves, seldom exceeding 15 cm in height. The margins of the leaves are rolled, and they are rusty and densely-hairy beneath. This plant is strongly aromatic when crushed — walking over a carpet of Labrador tea is quite an experience for anyone from a city — one's lungs feel newly reborn, cleansed!

When it is in full bloom, the white flowers of Labrador tea look like small explosions over the surface of the tundra. They occur in terminal clusters, each flower with 5 petals and 10 prominent stamens.

To recognize Labrador tea after the flowers fade, look for the typical leaves, crush one to obtain the characteristic scent, and look for the chestnut brown capsules, abruptly bent at the pedicel.

Many authors suggest that Labrador tea can be used as a tea, but, BEWARE! The foliage contains a toxin, ledol, which causes cramps and paralysis; this genus should *not* be used as a tea. (Johnson, 1987)

Labrador Tea Ona mikak eghotin kakoktanik naotialik. Kagaktitaotiton ilivakton hongayaknaini atongaoyam. Tonmagangata hapkoat atongaoyait tipait mamakhivaktot. Hela onatagangami.

Akoiyuktoni, himiyuktonilo, nanigijaiyoktonilo teliuyuktait hakoat eghotin, Bogiktomik imanmik kovigahogit atongaoyain, naotiangitlo. Ehohitelogo peyuktait. Ehotit hapkoat imaiton "ledol" pekagamik. Ehohitekpalakat, niukakpalagangatalo omatinon nakongitot, kayumikhinaktotlo, atongitkoni nakotgaik.

Lapland Rosebay
Rhododendron lapponicum

This is one of the most colorful of the tundra plants. It blooms early in the summer, in late June and early July in our area, and causes great areas to become pink in color.

The Lapland rosebay is a woody shrub, but seldom exceeds 10 cm in height in the central arctic, though it may grow taller in protected places. The branches and undersides of the leaves are covered with scurfy brown scales, and the somewhat oval, leathery leaves are spotted with scales on top. The margins of the leaves are rolled under, and the leaves generally seem to occur in clusters at the ends of the branches. The fragrant blooms are borne in a terminal cluster of four to eight pink to magenta flowers. White color phases of this plant are occasionally found.

The genus *Rhododendron* is an interesting one — it occurs on acid soils at high altitudes around the world, forming tangled forests in the Great Smoky Mountains of the U.S., and in the Himalayas. The rhododendrons typically grow on acid soils, but *R. lapponicum* does not; it usually occurs on limestone soils, which are basic. Individual plants intertwine to form a thick mat.

Labrador Tea *Ledum decumbens* / Sam Kapolak

Ledum decumbens / Sam Kapolak

Lapland Rosebay *Rhododendron lapponicum*
Sam Kapolak

Rhododendron lapponicum, white

Some authors state that *R. lapponicum* can be used to make a tea, but, since the genus *Rhododendron* contains the poisonous andromedotoxin, this is *not* recommended.

Lapland Rosebay Ona naotiat pinigiyaoyukton. Koyaginak hapkoat naoyokton, tavanga Great Smoky Mountinmi, tahamani U.S.mitomi, avongalo Eurapiyanmon tavongalo Himalayasmon. Chinamitomi elani tahiyukton malgoton iglobaton. Talgohiyukton hapkoat atongaoyat, behokvihaihotik.

Ovagot mikigaloahoni napatonoaton itot. Atongoayat ilangik takolikpagongnahaitit hamani nunami, ilangik ingliganitangokton. Naotiat hapkoat aopajalakotiyukton nunami Julaingogangat.

 Blueberry, Bog Bilberry, Kegotangenak
Vaccinium uliginosum

There are many species of blueberries, but the most common on the arctic coast is *Vaccinium uliginosum*. It is a low-growing shrub that is often almost prostrate due to wind pruning. The dull green leaves are oval, thin and flexible with smooth margins. They often appear reddish toward the margins, especially early and late in the summer, perhaps due to a concentration of pigments to allow photosynthesis when light levels are lower. The leaves become maroon in the fall.

The flowers are small pink-to-reddish bells borne in the axils of the leaves. These develop quickly into light green berries, which ripen to a deep blue. The surface of the berries is covered with a whitish "bloom" which can be rubbed off. The berries are juicy, with a delicate sweet taste. They are far tastier than the cultivated varieties of blueberry.

The main use of blueberries, for food and flavoring, is obvious. Besides using them fresh, the Inuit of the central arctic often preserved them in seal oil or fat, adding fish or meat when eating them. This practice has virtually died out, now. Blueberry leaves are used by the Dene to make a tea, and for medicinal purposes (sore throat and gums). The fruits are an important food of bears in the fall, and many birds, such as gulls and grey jays, feed on them.

In the more recent botanical literature, the genus *Vaccinium* is often now put into a separate family, the Vacciniaceae.

Kegotangenak Hapkoat mamagiyaoyut hamani. Ilitanatok hapkoat kegotanginak. Ilitogivakpigik kegotanginak naotiangik, aopayaklokton, aopajalakivakton, hivayakotiton itot.

Kegotanginak hapkoat ayunangiton kanok atogaihanik. Egalogik pailiuklugitlo, avokhaliuhugitlo, milahiliuhogitlo, mokbaoyamotlonit, onaktomotlonit itoktotinot, alupimonlonit avogiyuktait, mikigotigiblogitlo.

Blueberry
Vaccinium uliginosum, flowers

Vaccinium uliginosum / Sam Kapolak

Vaccinium uliginosum / Sam Kapolak

Vaccinium uliginosum / J. Irons

Lingonberry, Mountain Cranberry, Rock Cranberry, Kinminak
Vaccinium vitis-idaea

Another important berry-producing plant is the lingonberry, or mountain cranberry. It is a prostrate plant that rarely exceeds 5 cm in height. The evergreen leaves are oval, with edges rolled under, and a shiny upper surface.

Flowers are small white-to-pink bells borne at the tips of the branches. As sunlight passes through the fused petals that form the bell, it warms the air inside the bell. Due to the fact that warm air rises, this air stays inside the bell, remaining in place around the ovaries. This raises the temperature of the tissue slightly, just enough to assist in the formation of the fruit during the brief arctic summer.

The fruit of the lingonberry is a firm berry that persists on the plant throughout the winter. It does not fully ripen until after the first frosts, but can be picked before ripening. The berries begin white, turn a bright red, and ripen to a maroon color. The texture is mealy, and they are quite tart before being frozen. It is always a thrill to realize that these berries are at their most tasty (for eating off the plant) after having passed the long winter under the snow. There are few other berries around in the spring, and they are deeply appreciated by the Inuit at that time.

The scientific name of this plant "vitis-idaea" means "vine of Mt. Ida", derived from the name of a mountain in Greece. Lingonberries are commercially harvested in Europe, especially in Scandinavia.

In the late summer and fall, the lingonberry plants, especially those in areas receiving some shade, form odd fleshy red leaves at the tips of some branches. This is apparently an adaptation to continue photosynthesis when light levels are lower (Willard and Zwinger, 1972).

Kinminak Onataot baongat mamagiyaoyuktok. Kinmingnat okoat nunainakmi naotiyokton, nevegayuktotlo oyakani. Aopajalakiyukton Ausgusingogangat nunaptini, aonahayukton kehemi, okaingogangat aoyukton. Aongikalaokhotit pokuinagailik, atungitpata ilingnagialik kekomavingmot. Aopajalakiyukton egagpata.

Kegotanginaktot itotaot, kinmingnatlo koyagingnaktaot atuyuktait. Avoliuhogitlo, ilpkalogitlo, juisiliukhogitlo, mobaoyamotlo atoyuktait. Inupiat tavanikmuitan akoplogit atuyutait, kalikongmot nanokhogit, nimiklogo kongohinikmot igailiugangat havaotigiyuktait.

Mountain Cranberry
Vaccinium vitis-idaea.

Vaccinium vitis-idaea

Vaccinium vitis-idaea / Sam Kapolak

Vaccinium vitis-idaea

Alpine Azalea
Loiseleuria procumbens

This is a plant of the high wind-swept ridges, and exposed places. It is a woody plant, as are most of the Ericaceae, but forms a low mat, closely pressed to the ground. Snow sifts down into the intertwined leaves and twigs, and forms a protective drift over the entire plant, protecting the tender twigs from wind pruning.

The leathery leaves of this plant are less than 4 mm long, with a waxy, shiny surface, an adaptation that reduces loss of water from the plant tissues. The bell-shaped pink flowers are have five petals, which form a star shape. They do not bend over (as do the flowers of many other members of the heath family), but are raised above the surface of the plant on short red pedicels. The plant is insect-pollinated.

Alpine Azalea Ona naotiak mikanoanik oblogaiton itonik naotialik, hatonik hongayaktonik atongaoyalik. Hapkoat naotiyokton anogikanikmi okiomi. Anogimi Keyovaliuyaktanimi naotiyokton. Okoat naotiyokton manikami, tagiovalonilo. Nunami ikitoni.

Alpine Azalea
Loiseleuria procumbens
Sam Kapolak

Loiseleuria procumbens

Epilobium augustifolium / Sam Kapolak

Miscellaneous

- Thrift
  Armeria maritima
- Gentiana arctophila
- Gentiana propinqua
- Gentiana tenella
- Marsh felwort
  Lomatogonium rotatum
- Seaside bluebells
  Mertensia maritima
- Butterwort
  Pinguicula sp.
- Arctic harebell
  Campanula uniflora
- Tall fireweed
  Epilobium angustifolium
- Broad-leafed willowherb
  Epilobium latifolium
- Flax
  Linum lewisii
- Large-flowered wintergreen
  Pyrola grandiflora
- Side-flowered wintergreen
  Pyrola secunda
- Diapensia lapponica
- Rock-jasmine
  Androsace chamaejasme
- Primula stricta
- Fairy candelabra
  Androsace septentrionalis

PLUMBAGINACEAE LEADWORT FAMILY

This alpine/arctic family is characterized by clusters of flowers on slender stalks. It has only one representative in the central arctic, *Armeria maritima.*

Thrift
Armeria maritima

Armeria maritima is a distinctive looking plant — it has a tight round head of pink flowers at the tip of a long scape, and a cluster of thin, linear leaves at the base. Each flower seems to sit in a cup of papery tan bracts, and the whole cluster looks like a miniature bouquet of strawflowers. When they emerge, the flowers are quite red, and make the whole flower head appear reddish. When they are fully open, however, the flowers are pink. The basal calyx bracts persist after the seeds drop, making it possible to locate these plants in late fall or after the snow melts in spring.

On first glance, *A. maritima* could be confused with wild chives (*Allium* sp.). However, the leaves do not smell like onions, and the flower head is quite different — that of the wild chive has an umbel of flowers on pedicels all arising at a common center, no papery calyx bracts. To my knowledge, the wild chive reaches the arctic coast no further east than the the Coppermine area.

Thrift is circumpolar and very common in alpine areas in Europe, where it is frequently cultivated as a rock garden plant.

Thrift Ona atongaoyak koyaginak naotiyoktok. Aopajakloktok naotiagit, mokpakton ilainani napavaini naoyokton. Naotiagit katagagangamik olumihiyutiyukton, tetegangmik havakhimayuton.

GENTIANACEAE • GENTIAN FAMILY

These are some of the last flowers to bloom in the arctic summer. There are two genera in our area, *Gentiana* and *Lomatogonium*. *Gentiana* is named after Gentius, an herbalist king of Illyria in the 2nd century B.C.

This family is characterized by some of the most beautiful blue colors to be found in the plant kingdom. In the central arctic, all three of the local gentians bloom at the same time, together, on sandy beaches where the sand is fairly stable, and not blown much. They are so small that they can easily be missed, but so lovely that, once you have seen them, you tend to remember where they bloomed and look for them ever after.

Some authors have revised the genus *Gentiana*, leaving in this genus only a series of tall plants with spotted purple or yellow flowers, which occur only in Europe. However, since we are following the taxonomy outlined in Porsild & Cody (1980), we will retain the genus name *Gentiana* in this book.

Thrift *Armeria maritima*

Armeria maritima

Gentiana arctophila and G. propinqua

These are delicate little gentians that grow along the sandy shores on the arctic coast. They seldom exceed 10 - 12 cm in height. They are closely related. At first glance, you can tell they are "four-sided", as the blooms are obviously square when viewed from above. They look just like miniature rockets ready to fire. The flowers are a clear purplish-blue that does not photograph correctly (they seem too purple in most photographs). The stem and leaves are a reddish purple; basal leaves are about the same length as the flowers, approximately 2 - 2.5 cm long.

G. arctophila and *G. propinqua* are similar, but *G. propinqua* has a bristlelike tip to the petals; *G. arctophila* does not. In flower, *G. arctophila* is smaller than *G. propinqua*, but this is not a reliable characteristic. The distribution of *G. propinqua* more-or-less follows the treeline; it is a boreal forest plant; while *G. arctophila* is arctic. The ranges overlap in the area to the east of the Mackenzie delta.

Some authors now place *G. arctophila* (and *G. propinqua*) in the genus *Gentianella*.

Gentiana propinqua Onataok mikak atongaoyak hiugakaningmitaot naotiyoktok, tagioganikmi haniani. Naotiangit hongayakton, hitamanik begakton. Ehiviogitogaloak, ehiviotiagoni kehemi pinitaktok.

 Gentiana tenella

This small gentian has clear light blue flowers, and light green, tender foliage, tinged with reddish brown. It is approximately 15 cm high, but begins flowering at approximately 5 cm, so this height may be misleading. Take a hand-lens and look into the flowers — you will see a delicate fringing in the throat.

G. tenella is an annual, and blooms on sandy beaches and mudflats along the coast of the Arctic Ocean. Annuals are relatively rare in arctic regions. They have to grow from seed, flower and set seed in one short season.

This species has been placed in the genus *Comastoma* [the name means "fringed" (*coma*) "opening" (*stoma*)] by some taxonomists, and in *Gentianella* by others. It apparently has no common name, though the name "Lapland gentian" may apply to this plant.

Gentiana tenella Ona ahitkohongoyat atongaoyak nuna egingitkoni. Mikanoanik hongayaktonoanik naotialik, hongayaktonik atongaoyalik, hiugakanikmi naotiyokton hinani nunaptini. Koyaginak naotiyuitok.

Gentiana propinqua

Gentiana tenella

Marsh Felwort
Lomatogonium rotatum

This is another member of the gentian family that can easily be missed. It is quite memorable, however, because it blooms so late, when the "rush" of arctic flowers is over, and because it is such a lovely color.

L. rotatum is a small (5 to 20 cm) annual or biennial with reddish or purplish stem and leaves. Its flowers do not resemble typical gentian flowers. They are purplish in bud, but open to reveal the lovely sky blue color of the inner sides of the petals. In the early stages of bloom, the purplish sepals remain closed, giving the impression that there is a reddish purple center to the flower. These finally reflex, exposing the stamens and pistil.

Lomatogonium begins blooming while quite small, producing a single flower. This is likely the first year plant. In the second year, it is much taller, with several flowers.

Marsh Felwort Onataot atongaoyak allagayuk hiugakanimi naotiyoktok, tagioganikmi. Ona taktok kehemi piniktonit hongayaktonik naotialik napavaini. Ungmayukton obogaiton kilak ajikohikhogo.

BORAGINACEAE • BORAGE FAMILY

This large family, which includes the forget-me-nots and the lungworts, has only one representative in our area, *Mertensia maritima.*

Seaside Bluebells, Sea Lungwort
Mertensia maritima

Seaside bluebells are prostrate and grow on the shore, often very close to the water's edge, certainly within the range of a lot of salt spray. It is a true halophyte, or "salt-lover", in that it can tolerate conditions that would discourage most plants. It has a wide range, occurring from the coast of Alaska and Siberia across to northern Europe.

M. maritima is a striking plant, with or without its flowers. It is a fleshy, succulent plant which stores water in the tissues of its grey-green leaves. It sprawls on the rocks, taking advantage of the relatively calm zone close to the ground, and often occurs on the fissured surface of algal limestone islands, sandstone islands, or gravelly beaches. The grey-green leaves are the first thing you notice about this plant — they are oval or spoon-shaped, and 3 - 5 mm thick. The plant is sometimes called "oyster plant" because its leaves taste quite fishy. They are not utilized by the Inuit, however.

The flowers remind one of those of the Virginia bluebells of the south (they are of the same genus) — they are bell-shaped, and, when in bud, are pinkish, changing to a delicate light blue as the flower matures. White variants are rare, but do occur.

Marsh Felwort
Lomatogonium rotatum

Seaside Bluebells *Mertensia maritima*

Mertensia maritima / Sam Kapolak

This flower is a photographer's nightmare, as it "fluoresces", causing a shift in color (toward purple) when the image is recorded on film.

The seeds are nutlets inside a light green, spongy outer coating. They float on water, which aids in their dispersal to other shores.

Seaside Bluebell Hapkoataot atongaoyat oyagalaini naotiyukton, tagioganikmi imami. Atongaoyain hongayaklokton, ivyunik atongaoyalging. Atongaoyaini imakmik ilipkayuton. Baniumanikmi naotiyokton, tagiomik pilimaitok, imaigotihakhongogamik tagiogtogan. Ona oktogok atongaoyak, ekalukton tipilik.

LENTIBULARIACEAE
BLADDERWORT FAMILY

This family contains the butterworts and bladderworts, both carnivorous plants, capable of digesting the protein of insects or aquatic invertebrates.

Butterwort
Pinguicula sp.

These small plants have a spurred purple flower borne on a slender stem, and a basal rosette of yellowish-green leaves with sticky surfaces. Small insects are trapped on the surface of the leaves. The insect tissues are broken down by digestive enzymes secreted by the plant, and the nutrients are absorbed into the leaf surface. Take a look at the leaves of these tiny plants (use a hand lens), and you will see the remains of many small insects stuck to the leaf. Under a low-power microscope, you can see the droplets of digestive enzymes on the leaf surface.

Butterworts grow in boggy areas, especially at the edges of minute tundra ponds, on calcareous soil or in carpets of sphagnum moss. In these boggy areas, the nitrogen compounds are chemically trapped, and unavailable to plants. By utilizing insect protein, the plant is able to take advantage of a supplemental source of nitrates.

There are two butterworts in our area. Largest and most common is *Pinguicula vulgaris*, which has tongue-shaped leaves approximately 2.5 cm in length. The leaves of *P. villosa* are much smaller, less than 1 cm in length, and blunt-tipped, with a distinct groove down the middle. The flower of *P. vulgaris* is about 1.5 cm across, while that of *P. villosa* is less than .5 cm across. *P. vulgaris* almost always occurs on moist calcareous soil, while *P. villosa* grows in mats of sphagnum, often at the margins of tiny tundra pools.

It's quite a thrill to discover these minute plants, and this points up the importance of looking closely at all around you. We often hike over the vast expanse of the tundra world with our attention fixed on the distance, on a caribou, a soaring hawk, or a mineral outcropping. Take time to look closely, and you will discover another world in a jewel-like puddle on a tundra slope — a world of minute plants, of mosquito larvae, and wolf spiders bearing the precious burdens of their egg sacs.

Pinguicula villosa

Butterwort
Pinguicula vulgaris / Sam Kapolak

Pinguicula vulgaris

Butterwort Ona atongaoyak angonahoayuktok, negeyuktok kiktogainik, milogainik, koyaginaklo mikanoanik tingmiyuktonik. Maliyuitait, opakiyuitaitlo. Kogitain atongaoyait napavaini nipikanaktomik pilik, imaton kiktogainik koyaginaklo nekegeyuktait. Mikanoat tingmiyukton ovonga atongaoyakmon mitgangata nipiyukton, nekoayukton omoga atongaoyamot. Ona atongaoyak kinipanikmi naotiyoktok, imaitokokinikmi nitrogenmik. Tingmiyuktonik mikaknik negegangamik nitrogeniyukton.

Ona hongayavyaktok ehiviotaigok naotiagik, tonoani takohaoyuk ipiktonoak nipikanaktok talvani pehimayutait, nagaiyuktait ona mikan tingmiyukton.

CAMPANULACEAE *BLUEBELL AND HAREBELL FAMILY*

This family includes the bellflowers, sheepsbits, rampions, and the harebells, many plants that have been cultivated as rock-garden plants the world over. Almost all members of the family are a clear blue to purplish blue.

Arctic Harebell, Single-Flowered Harebell
Campanula uniflora

This small (less than 10 cm tall) harebell blooms in late July in our area. It grows on well-drained calcareous soil and gravel slopes, and on ancient strandlines. The leaves are lanceolate and somewhat leathery, about 5 cm long. The clear blue flowers are nodding, with petals slightly outcurved, not as clearly bell-shaped as some other members of this genus. Instead, they are almost funnel-shaped.

The genus name, "Campanula", is derived from the Latin *campana*, meaning "a bell". The specific epithet, *uniflora* means "one-flowered". These do resemble minute bells decorating the low tundra, like specks of the sky captured on the land.

Harebell Ona mikak atongaoyak, toatonik atongaoyalik, hongayaktonik naotialik ahigotatonoak, naoyoktok kehemi anogikangnikmi. Hapkoat naotiat anogi hogiyiutat, napavin kitonamik anogimi nakoyun.

ONAGRACEAE • EVENING-PRIMROSE OR WILLOWHERB FAMILY

The evening-primrose family is a family of large and showy flowers. They have four petals and four sepals, and could be mistaken for mustards, but the ones in our area are so readily recognizable that there is little confusion. The ovary is inferior (below the base of the petals and sepals), forming a long tubelike structure between the petals and the base of the flower. This capsule elongates as the seeds mature, but does not push out through the flower as does the silique of the mustards.

Arctic Harebell
Campanula uniflora

Campanula uniflora

Tall Fireweed
Epilobium angustifolium

A characteristic flower of the North, fireweed is the territorial flower of the Yukon. It is common in disturbed areas and on burns south of the treeline, but is less common on the arctic coast.

The flowers, in a tall raceme, are a conspicuous rose-pink, 2 - 3 cm in diameter, with 4 petals and 4 slightly darker sepals, which extend out alternately with the petals rather than being concealed behind them. The bottom flowers bloom first, and the bloom proceeds up the stalk. Seeds form in a long capsule, which splits laterally, releasing the seeds with their long silky white tufts, to be dispersed by the winds of autumn.

The leaves are narrow, lance-shaped, dark green on top and paler beneath. This is one of our tallest flowers, reaching a meter in height, and is one of the last flowers to bloom in our area.

The tall fireweed reaches the limits of its range on the arctic coast, and does not occur on the arctic islands unless seeds are transported there by aircraft (a quite likely occurrence, since fireweed is common on airports in the southern N.W.T.).

E. angustifolium has recently been removed from the genus *Epilobium* and placed in the genus *Chamerion* (Weber, 1987). Several New World species have been redefined based on evidence that they are the same as species described from the Old World (Europe).

Tall Fireweed Ona piniktok aopayakyukitok naotiat ulamniknaitok naotiani. Taghitayuktok angotim hilviaganot. Algakhimaningmi naotiyokton nunami. Atikhimayon "Ekoalakhimayot ivik." Naohimagamik ekoalakhimavatomi nunami. Ona naotiat atoktaoyuktok pinikotigiblogo avani Britinmi, Eurapiyamiolo.

Broad-Leafed Willowherb, Dwarf Fireweed, River Beauty
Epilobium latifolium

This is the truly arctic fireweed, with a range extending into the arctic archipelago and around the coast of Greenland. It is more common than the tall fireweed in our area, growing on sandy or gravelly damp shores, often in areas where the soil has been disturbed.

The flowers do not form tall racemes, but loose, broad clusters. They are large (2 - 5 cm across) and very showy — with four broad rose pink to purplish petals alternating with 4 slightly darker sepals. The white-tufted seeds are similar to those of the tall fireweed, but the pods are not as long.

The leaves of the dwarf fireweed are greyish green, almost oval in shape, and somewhat fleshy. The young leaves and stalks, shoots, and flowers of both the fireweeds were used as salad herbs and pot-herbs by the early explorers. (See Walker, 1984.)

Epilobium latifolium has also been shifted to the genus *Chamerion* in recent years, so in literature written later than the mid-1980s, it may be called *Chamerion latifolium*.

Tall Fireweed
Epilobium angustifolium

Epilobium latifolium / J. Irons

Dwarf Fireweed *Epilobium latifolium*

Dwarf Fireweed Ona atongaoyak naikaik, takikaini, naotiagitlo angitkait. Atia "river beauty" imaton kokap pinikota, naotiyokamik tolonikmi hiukami, oyagavalaikmilo kokani. Atongaoyait mayavakton, hongayahotik. Nutak atongaoyait, napavitlo egatatait nekilaimot avogiyuktait, egahimaitomiklonit. Atutaoginatok Alaskamiunit inupianin. Ketka napavai akitoa negeyuktait, atongaoyaitoak teliuhugik. Hapkoat naotiat atuyuitavot nunaptini, ahini atuktoayukhoni koyaginak.

LINACEAE • _FLAX FAMILY_

Throughout history, the flax family has been of tremendous economic importance, as a source of linseed oil, linen, and medicines. Linen is a fine fabric woven of thread which is spun from fiber extracted from the stems of flax plants. As a matter of fact, the term "linen" comes from _Linum_, the genus name for flax.

Flax
Linum lewisii

This delicate and beautiful flower is not common in the central arctic, but is such a treat to find that we've included it. It is recorded from the Mackenzie delta, Bathurst Inlet area, and western Victoria Island.

Flax is a relatively tall plant for our area, producing several leafy stems 15 to 20 cm in height. The leaves are linear, 1 - 2 cm long, arranged alternately on the stem. The flowers are the real surprise — they are fairly large (2 - 2.5 cm across), and a lovely pale blue. They begin blooming with petals folded into a trumpet shape, but open flat. At the same time, the stalks tend to drop down to lie parallel to the ground, so the plant looks like the centre of a wheel, with the spokes radiating from the hub, each ending with an aquamarine jewel. The flowers last only a couple days. The ovaries expand to form globular capsules, with two large seeds in each chamber or locule.

Flax Ona atongaoyak koyaginak nunami naoyokton, ilagiyaik tapkoat ivaloliuyoktait, kalicohaliugaloahogolo atongaoyat. Napavin naotiagiyoktait, kaogohogit napavin, hongayanai beyayuktait. Kaogagominaita ivaloliuyoktait.

Flax *Linum lewisii* / David Middleton

PYROLACEAE · WINTERGREEN FAMILY

This family is characterized by beautiful, low growing herbs with leaves clustered close to the base of the plant, in many cases resembling a basal rosette. It has showy, often waxy, flowers.

Although one would expect the leaves to smell of wintergreen, they do not. Oil of wintergreen is produced in plants in the genus *Gaultheria*, the teaberries. When the heath family was revised, *Pyrola* and related plants were removed and placed in the wintergreen family, while *Gaultheria* remained in the Ericaceae.

Large-Flowered Wintergreen
Pyrola grandiflora

In this attractive plant, a reddish stalk (10 - 15 cm) arises from a basal rosette of leathery evergreen leaves with prominent whitish veins. The stalk bears a raceme of sweet-scented creamy white flowers, each with 5 petals, 5 sepals, and 8 - 10 prominent yellow stamens. The flowers are relatively large, up to 2 cm in diameter, and face the ground when they open, rotating to face horizontally as they mature. Flowers give way to spherical reddish seed capsules.

The large-flowered wintergreen is very common in some areas along the coast and inland to Great Bear Lake, spangling the ground under willows in some coastal areas. It is usually at the peak of its bloom in mid-July.

Large Flowered Wintergreen Ona atongaoyak angiyunik naotialik. Keyoni atani naotyoktok. Atiani ona tipikanahogehongoyat, anokhiktoton nongolaton atikagamik. Tipikangitok, ogtogonilonit anokhingitok, ajikotagigaloahogo anokhitok naotiat, anikhiktomik ogholiuyuitok, taimatot nongolat anokhilakilikpaktot. Atongaoyait hongayanginaktot okiomi. Kokohegangat kiktogainit, kaogahogit atongaoyait kokokhinikmon nanuyoktait.

Side-Flowered Wintergreen
Pyrola secunda

This wintergreen is smaller than *P. grandiflora*, and easy to distinguish. It has oval evergreen leaves, emerging close to the base of the plant. The whole plant seldom exceeds 8 cm in height, and all flowers are borne on one side of the scape (stem). The scentless yellowish-green flowers are less than 1 cm across, and partially closed into a rounded bell shape, with the pistil extending well beyond the petals. The oval leaves have slightly pointed tips, and blunt teeth along their margins.

Large-flowered Wintergreen
Pyrola grandiflora / Sam Kapolak

Pyrola grandiflora

Side-flowered Wintergreen
Pyrola secunda

159

The side-flowered wintergreen also grows under willows, but does not occur in huge colonies. Look for it amid the large-flowered species; it is equally lovely in its own small way.

Side-flowered Wintergreen Ona atongaoyak mikatatkaik, angitkainit. Naotiagik iklovahiktot atavaini. Tipaitot hapkoat atongaoyat.

DIAPENSIACEAE

There is only one representative of this family in the central arctic, *Diapensia lapponica*, which grows on high windswept ridges. It is totally exposed to the elements, perhaps more than any other flowering plant, besides the purple mountain saxifrage.

 Diapensia lapponica

This little plant has adopted the mat growth habit; it forms tight mats on the ground, less than 1.5 cm in height. This is a protection against the abrasive forces of wind-driven snow. It is a woody plant, but the branches are concealed by the evergreen leaves. The leaves are about 1 cm in length, shiny, and somewhat spoon-shaped, with a groove along the midrib. They are dark green in summer, but fade to bronze in fall. It has no common name.

The showy white flowers (about 1-1.5 cm across) arise from the cushion on stout pedicels. They contrast with the tundra background, making it possible for their pollinators, bumble bees and flies, to locate them. Nothing is easy about life in this habitat, high on the ridges. When the wind is calm and the sun beats down, it is a baking desert. When clouds curl about the ridges, and the wind sweeps out of the northwest, rain can turn to sleet in an instant, all colors disappear, and winter seems but a breath away. One must admire the plants that cling to life in this environment — they are made of stern stuff.

Diapensia Ona atongaoyak naoyoktok kolvani imnavaloni, anogigoktonikmi okiomi apotailikpaktoni. Iliktot naotiyokton nunami, atongaoyait naniktiplotik nunamot. Naotiagit anguit kakoktaoplotit, napayun. Egotanit, neviovangnitlo mikataviovakton allanot mikatahotik, iblaoliutoton iliuyukton, imakton naotaihanik naotigiplotik.

Diapensia lapponica

PRIMULACEAE · PRIMROSE FAMILY

The primrose family (which includes the primroses, cowslips, rock-jasmines, snowbells, and cyclamens) has been cultivated in rock gardens since Elizabethan times. It occurs from the mountains of Asia to the Alps of Europe, and from the Rockies to the Brooks Range and the arctic coast in North America. The family includes some extremely showy plants, but in the central arctic, there are only a few.

Rock-Jasmine
Androsace chamaejasme

This gorgeous little primrose occurs in the western part of our region, as far east as Coppermine and the western part of Banks and Victoria Islands, and has been found near Cambridge Bay. It also occurs in Europe and Asia, and probably moved into our area from across the Bering Straits, after the retreat of the glaciers.

Its white flowers with yellow "eyes" are larger than the flowers of the other local primroses; they are usually 8 - 10 mm in diameter. These fragrant flowers are borne in an umbel on a sturdy stem 2 - 15 cm tall. A basal rosette of small, narrow, overlapping leaves puts out slender stolons which root to produce additional plants. In ideal habitat, the rosettes of rock-jasmine may form mats up to 15 cm across.

Primula stricta

This small but lovely flower is often trampled underfoot because it grows along shores where most people are concentrating on the fishing rather than the plants.

The small white-to-lilac flowers are composed of five deeply notched petals fused into a tube at the base. These are arranged in a solitary tight umbel of five to eight flowers at the tip of a long scape (10 - 20 cm) arising from a rosette of spoon-shaped basal leaves.

Primula egaliksensis also occurs in the central arctic, and is very similar to *P. stricta*. The flowers are lilac, but, since the flowers of *P. stricta* can also be lilac, this is a problem. Take a hand lens and check the calyx (the cuplike structure at the base of the flower) of all the lilac *Primulas* you find. The ones with minute threadlike projections on the lobes of the calyx are *P. egaliksensis*; those without are *P. stricta*. Wish you'd kept fishing?

Primrose Hapkoatlo mikanoat atongaoyat hinana naotiyokton. Atongaoyagaikton napavini, kakoktanik, hongayatoniklo naotialgit, kogitanik ketkalgit.

Rock-jasmine
Androsace chamaejasme / Pat Thagard

Primula stricta

Primula egalikensis (prob.)

Fairy Candelabra,
Northern Androsace, Pygmy Flower
Androsace septentrionalis

One to several small umbels of 5 to 12 flowers (apiece) arise from a basal rosette of green or reddish-green lanceolate leaves, which may have entire or toothed margins. The scape, umbel, and calyx of each flower may be green or red, and the flowers are white with a reddish cast.

One would assume from the apparent fragility of this flower that it would be extremely limited in its range or habitat, but this is not so; it is at home in the alpine areas of Europe, on gravel shores of islands on the arctic coast, eskers along arctic rivers, and at the edge of a parking lot in Yellowknife!

This minute but delicately beautiful little flower is an immense challenge to photograph. It is almost impossible to keep the leaves and the flowers in focus, due to the size of the plant, and shallow depth-of-field at the necessary magnification. The use of a flash can help by allowing you to use a smaller aperture, thus increasing the depth-of-field.

The similar *Androsace chamaejasme*, or rock jasmine, is shorter than *A. septentrionalis*, has larger flowers (8-10 mm across, as compared to 5 mm), and is not reddish in color, the flowers are white with yellow centres, and are quite fragrant.

Fairy Candelabra Piniktonoak ona atongaoyak, ilitoginiatok piniktok ingikovit haniani oyakami. Ona atongaoyak Europemilo naotiyoktok, imaton atiktoahimayuk "fairy candelabra" ekomatip tongavaiton. Atongaoyait ekomaviup tongavaiton inamik, naotiagiklo ekomatiton inamik.

Fairy Candelabra *Androsace septentrionalis*

Androsace septentrionalis

Lupinus arcticus, Pedicularis capitata

Paintbrushes & Louseworts

- Paintbrush
  Castilleja sp.

- Arctic lousewort
  Pedicularis arctica

- Capitate lousewort
  Pedicularis capitata

- *Pedicularis flammea*

- Woolly lousewort
  Pedicularis lanata

- Labrador lousewort
  Pedicularis labradorica

- Lapland lousewort
  Pedicularis lapponica

- Sudetan lousewort
  Pedicularis sudetica

SCROPHULARIACEAE
FIGWORT FAMILY

This family is an interesting one with many representatives in the arctic. It includes some of the world's most decorative garden plants, such as the snapdragons, foxgloves, toadflaxes, veronicas, eyebrights, rattles, Indian paintbrushes, and louseworts.

The Indian paintbrushes (genus *Castilleja*) and louseworts (genus *Pedicularis*) are, to some extent, semi-parasitic on the roots of grasses and woody plants, so are difficult to transplant, since they may not be able to establish a host-parasite relationship in the new area.

The "scrophs" as they are nicknamed, are highly evolved to take advantage of insects as pollinators. Their flower shapes seem specifically designed to entice insects to visit, and to ensure pollination.

 ## Paintbrush, Painted-Cup
Castilleja sp.

These colorful flowers brighten the tundra, blooming along with the lupines, creating great drifts of color that look like they have been "painted" across the land.

Nothing else looks like a paintbrush in flower, so there is no problem in recognizing the genus. However, identifying the paintbrushes to species is another matter! Porsild and Cody (1980) report both *Castilleja elegans* and *C. caudata* (revised from *C. pallidans*) in the central arctic. Some authors consider both these to be a subspecies of *C. pallidans*, and things get more confused from there!

It is my private opinion that these, if they are good species, need to be redefined. I think that they hybridize in our area. *C. caudata* is supposed to be yellowish to yellowish green (Porsild & Cody, 1980), and should have no hairs on stem and leaves. The leaves should be "caudate", i.e., having a long tail-like tip. *C. elegans* should be "violet-purple", and, by inference in Porsild and Cody's keys, should have hairs on stem and leaves. The leaves should not have a hair-like appendage at the tips. This doesn't work — there are plants that are white, with hairs on the stem; there are plants that have all sorts of leaf shapes, there are a whole range of colors from pink to quite a deep pink/magenta. There are very few that could be called "yellowish". Conclusion: For the purpose of this book, I would recommend that one call them just *Castilleja*, and wait until the botanists revise the genus!

At any rate, the paintbrushes are lovely, and have intricate, complicated flowers. Take a hand lens and have a close look. The actual flowers of this plant are arranged in a "head" and are nestled down behind colorful bracts. As the flower matures, the enlarging ovary pushes the green pistil out to where it can be seen. At its base, a set of stamens are clustered; these are usually pink to reddish, and must be passed by insects seeking nectar at the base of the pistil.

Paintbrush
Castilleja elegans / Sam Kapolak

Castilleja, white morph

Castilleja caudata

White variants are occasionally found. One, probably an albino, is illustrated. As you can see, there is no pigment in the flower, or the leaves. This particular plant probably survived to maturity and flowering because it is parasitic, and can live without chlorophyll.

Paintbrushes Hapkoat atongaoyat koyaginak naotiyokton nunami, naokatigiyuktait lupine. Kakoktaohongoyut, kogitaolotiklonit, aopayangajiklotiklonik, aopayalakiplotiklo.

Hapkoak nekekayukton allanit atongaoyanit napavin iloani nunamiton allanot napavinot pilikpagain, taimaton negelikpakamik, keyokton, iviktonlonit kokilikpakamik negainik.

LOUSEWORTS

The genus *Pedicularis* has a fascinating history. Its name, and the common name, "lousewort" (louse plant) are derived from an old story:

In Scotland, louseworts grew in fields with poor soil, fields used by peasants who kept low quality cattle. These animals were often unthrifty, and developed louse infestations. The story arose that the cattle caught the lice from the plants in the fields, and from this the plants acquired the name lousewort. The scientific name also reflects this — "pedicularis" means "little louse".

Like the paintbrushes, the louseworts are semi-parasitic. They often parasitize the roots of woody plants through root connections called "haustoria". However, they are not "obligate parasites" — most species do not have to be parasitic to survive.

The louseworts are fairly similar — many have a basal rosette of leaves which are often pinnately lobed, a central stalk, and irregular flowers in a spike-like inflorescence. The flowers are bilaterally (rather than radially) symmetrical. The calyx of each flower is tubular, and the corolla (whorl of petals) has two sections. The upper is compressed laterally to form a helmet that clasps and conceals the stamens and (partially) the pistil. The lower is flattened to create a landing platform for insects, and drops down under the weight of the insect to allow access to the nectary. At the same time, the pistil and/or stamens rotate downward to contact the insect's back. The Inuit call the louseworts, especially *P. arctica*, "bumblebee flowers", because they are visited by bumblebees.

Louseworts Hapkoak egotakmik atiktaohimayun, egotamin mitimavigiyukamigit. Aoyalihagangak mitimavigiyaoginakmak.

Naotiagit hilanmogayut napavaini. Naotiangit eliukpikton itot, tokhoangit ataini henaktomik pilgik. Egotan miyukton eliukpinon inoknaitonmik niukagaiganik henaktomit, ataotikot kahagakhogit kogitakanai naotiam, allamotaot mitgangat honaitot, kehemi nipitkanatok. Kogitakanai omoga nanokhogo, imaton naotiahumik piyuk.

Hapkoat koyaginak kalokakton, kogitaoplotin, aopayangajiplotinlo. Elaitaot maklongayumit aopayaktomiklo pikayukton.

KEY TO THE LOUSEWORTS

Keys have not often been used in this book, but, in the case of the louseworts, it makes life much easier. The following key will aid in their identification:

1. Stem branched; flowers yellow, with touch of reddish brown on back of helmet............... Labrador Lousewort *Pedicularis labradorica.*
    Stem not branched 2

2. Flowers yellow, cream-colored, or red and yellow 3
    Flowers pink or a combination of red and pink 6

3. Flowers yellow, helmets with brown or red to reddish purple on crest or apex 4
    Flowers yellow, with reddish brown on back of helmet, young plants that have not yet branched ....
    .... Labrador Lousewort *Pedicularis labradorica.*

4. Flowers yellow; helmets red to reddish purple; small plant, less than 12 cm, stem often red .... *Pedicularis flammea.*
    Flowers yellow or creamy yellow 5

5. Flowers pale yellow, arranged around the stem, within 3 cm of the top; stem (and sometimes leaves) reddish purple; helmet with a distinct beak .... Lapland Lousewort *Pedicularis lapponica.*
    Flowers creamy yellow, in "head" at apex of stem, all within 1.5 cm of top; stem tinged with red at the base, but not completely reddish; helmet lacking distinct beak, but has touch of red at the tip ....
    .... Capitate Lousewort *Pedicularis capitata.*

6. Flowers definitely bicolored red (helmet) and pink or whitish pink; flowers arranged in relatively tight head at apex of stem, though this may elongate as the bloom progresses; basal rosette of leaves, and relatively few leaves on the stem; resemble peppermint pinwheel candies from above .... Sudetan Lousewort *Pedicularis sudetica.*
    Flowers pink 7

7. Helmet prominently arched, bearing a tooth on each side, just before the apex where the pistil protrudes; plant usually with some hairs along the stem, but not emerging like a cotton tuft....................
    .... Arctic Lousewort *Pedicularis arctica.*
    Helmet curved but not prominently arched, lacks teeth; plant usually (but not always) emerging as a cottony tuft through which the flowers extend.............. Woolly Lousewort *Pedicularis lanata.*

Arctic Lousewort
Pedicularis arctica

The arctic lousewort is a fairly large, robust plant, often reaching 18 - 20 cm in height. Its flowers are a clear pink, with the lip slightly lighter than the helmet. Their diagnostic character is the presence of a pair of thin teeth, one on each side of the helmet, just before the apex. This character is important, if it is pink and has the teeth, it is *P. arctica*; if there are no teeth, it is probably *P. lanata*.

This lousewort has a pale yellow taproot; several flowering stems may arise from one taproot. Compared to *P. lanata*, it has relatively little hair, but those blooming early in the season do have some translucent hairs on the stems. Long leaves are mixed in with the flowers, often extending at least three times the length of the flowers.

Photographers take note — be sure to focus carefully to get the teeth - otherwise, you will have problems identifying your photos.

Some authors report that all parts of the arctic lousewort are edible, steamed as a potherb, but the Inuit do not use them. The Inuit children suck the nectar from the individual flowers.

Capitate Lousewort,
Few-Flowered Lousewort
Pedicularis capitata

This lousewort is easy to identify, since it is so different. The flowers are a creamy pale yellow with a brownish red dot on the helmet. There are only a few (usually 2 to 4), in a tight "head" at the apex of the stem, which usually bears only a few leaves. The plant is usually between 5 and 15 cm high.

P. capitata often occurs with arctic lupines on gravelly calcareous tundra. It is circumpolar in distribution, but does not occur around most of southern and eastern Greenland, nor around Hudson Bay.

Pedicularis flammea

P. flammea is a small lousewort, only reaching 5 to 10 cm in our area. The scentless flowers are bright yellow, almost orange, and the helmet is tipped with red to reddish purple, almost as if it had been dipped in paint. The lip of the flower is distinctly three-lobed. The stem is red, hairless, and with relatively few leaves; most leaves are in a basal rosette.

This plant is not very common on the arctic coast, but may have been overlooked, as it is so small. It has no common name, but "flammea" probably refers to the red tip to the helmet — "touched with flame."

Arctic Lousewort
Pedicularis arctica

Capitate Lousewort
Pedicularis capitata / Sam Kapolak

Pedicularis flammea

Woolly Lousewort
Pedicularis lanata

This is one of the "typical" plants of the tundra, the one people think of whenever they have to define "tundra". It is striking in all phases, from the time the stalk emerges from the ground until it produces seeds. It is truly amazing to walk over a wide expanse of tundra dotted all about with these little furballs!

P. lanata arises from a stout yellow taproot, and emerges from the ground as a rounded structure not unlike a mushroom, all covered in white translucent hairs. This soon elongates, and the bright pink flowers push through the heat-trapping hairs to unfold and attract insects. It is difficult to differentiate this lousewort from *P. arctica* — the flowers of the woolly lousewort are of a uniform pink, and lack the subapical tooth on the helmet. Also, there are relatively few long leaves poking out from among the flowers.

For a number of years, I thought that the arctic lousewort bloomed early in the summer, and that the woolly lousewort bloomed later, in August. Such is not the case, but the early-blooming woolly louseworts do not emerge as cute little rounded lollipops. They resemble *P. arctica* in that they are quite tall, but have a considerable amount of hair along the stem. Check the key for diagnostics.

A number of sources mention that the yellow taproot of *P. lanata* is tasty raw, boiled, baked, stir-fried, or steamed, and that the leaves and stems can also be steamed. The local Inuit do not use them. *P. lanata* is not a plant which produces harvestable plant parts — if any portion is picked, the plant dies. It seems a pity to destroy such a lovely plant for the sake of a taste.

Labrador Lousewort
Pedicularis labradorica

Another easy one — the Labrador lousewort is the only lousewort that has a branching stem. It is also pretty large, can reach 20 cm in our area. Though the branching stem is a good characteristic, remember that young individuals may produce a single stem, and then flower, thus negating the diagnostic characteristic.

The flowers of *P. labradorica* are yellow, with a brown crest on the helmet, extending almost the length of the helmet. The stem and leaves are often a purplish green.

Woolly Lousewort
Pedicularis lanata
David Middleton

Pedicularis lanata / Sam Kapolak

Pedicularis lanata root / Lorne Smith / GNWT

Labrador Lousewort *Pedicularis labradorica*

Lapland Lousewort
Pedicularis lapponica

A small lousewort, usually 8 - 12 cm, with fragrant pale yellow flowers in a fairly short "head". Foliage and stem are purplish brown. These little louseworts usually occur in moist depressions in dry tundra, and can grow in thick groups.

    P. lapponica occurs throughout the low arctic, but is not too common on the coast, seemingly preferring to grow inland. It is difficult to remember the differences between this species and the Labrador lousewort, although the branching characteristic is an obvious one. It has always helped me to think of the branching rivers of Labrador, and the branches of the Labrador lousewort — It's weak, but it works.

Sudetan Lousewort
Pedicularis sudetica

Named for Sudetanland, in Germany, this is one of the most attractive of the louseworts. From the top, it resembles a peppermint pinwheel candy, with the red stripes of the helmets radiating out from the center.

    Each flower is bicolored — the helmet is red, and the lip is white or pink with two rows of red spots down the center. As in *P. arctica*, there is a fine tooth on each side of the helmet, just before the apex. The flowers are closely clustered together at the top of the stalk in a somewhat white-woolly inflorescence, but this elongates as the bloom advances. The scape usually bears only one or two leaves, and there is a basal rosette of deeply-cut, pinnately lobed leaves.

    P. sudetica is a plant of stream and pond edges and marshy places, often growing right at the edge of the water. It often grows in association with arctic cotton, yellow marsh saxifrage, and the purple bladder-campion.

Lapland Lousewort *Pedicularis lapponica*

Pedicularis lapponica

Sudetan Lousewort *Pedicularis sudetica*

Pedicularis sudetica

Arnica at Bathurst Inlet

Composites

- Yarrow
  Achillea nigrescens
- Everlastings
  Antennaria spp.
- Alpine arnica
  Arnica alpina
- Aster
  Aster spp.
- Arctic daisy
  Chrysanthemum integrifolium
- Fleabane
  Erigeron sp.
- Sea-shore chamomile
  Matricaria ambigua
- Wormwood
  Artemisia tilesii
- Coltsfoot
  Petasites sagittatus
- Dwarf hawksbeard
  Crepis nana
- Fireworks flower
  Saussurea angustifolia
- Groundsel
  Senecio atropurpureus
- Black-tipped groundsel
  Senecio lugens
- Mastodon flower
  Senecio congestus
- Dandelion
  Taraxacum spp.

COMPOSITAE · COMPOSITES
SUNFLOWER OR DAISY FAMILY

This is one of the largest plant families. What appear to be "flowers" or "flowerheads" in this family are really many little flowers, closely packed together in a bunch, or "head". If you take an arctic daisy, and pull the flowerhead apart, you will find hundreds of tiny individual flowers perched on a flat or round-topped receptacle.

Each of the yellow or white "petals" around the outside of the daisy is an individual flower. The flat, colored part is the petal, and the other flower parts, such as the stamens and the pistil, are in the tube where the flower attaches to the base, or peduncle. These outer flowers are called "ray flowers" or ligulate (tongue-shaped) flowers. The short yellow centre of the daisy is also made up of many tiny flowers, called "disk flowers" or tube flowers. These disk flowers have stamens and/or pistils, but no obvious petals.

The seeds of most composites are spread by being blown in the wind, so they usually have some kind of wing or fluffy silk to catch the wind. Each tiny flower of a composite produces only one seed, so you can see how many flowers make up a dandelion by blowing on the seedhead. Sometime, take a dandelion seedhead apart, counting all the individual seeds.

Composite, Sunflower or Daisy Family Ona atongaoyak angiyuk. Naotiagit hapkoak atongaoyap naotiagaiton, naikokton iliplotik. Imaitonmik naotiatmik pilokligongni, ehiviotaigoni amigaitonit naotiagaiton.

Kakoktat, kogitatlonit naotiat hilataniton naotiamit, naotiagoyut. Piniknai oma atongaoyan, ilangatoat naotiap naotiangoyuk napavinmi, ataploni atongaoyanmot. Oma naotiap hilata ima taiyukta "ray flowers." Ketkanitaot kogitat naiton naotiagoyuntoat imaton taivagain "disk flowers." Angiunik kehemi atongaoyaiton.

Naotiahait hapkoak anokimit titkatayukton, imaton ehagolikton itot, anokimi titkatagaingani. Naotianoat hapkoa ataohinakmik naotiahamik piyuton. Hoblogongi ona naotiat takohongoyatin naotiagaikton ketkani.

Yarrow
Achillea nigrescens

The genus *Achillea* is common throughout the northern hemisphere; its members are called milfoils or sneezeworts. The leaves of yarrow are aromatic when crushed.

Our yarrow, *A. nigrescens*, is very similar to an introduced European yarrow (*A. millefolium*) that is common in Yellowknife and the south. However, the native species is smaller, and has relatively wide ray flowers; they are as broad as they are long, about 5 mm. Also, the scalelike involucral bracts (the overlapping scales that cover the base of the

Yarrow *Achillea nigrescens*
Sam Kapolak

Achillea nigrescens

flowerhead) have brown or black margins. The flowers of the yarrow are white to pinkish; they tend to become pinker with age. The ray and disk flowers are the same color.

A. nigrescens occurs on lake shores and sandy margins of rivers. The name is derived from the Latin *niger*, meaning "black", and refers to the margins of the bracts.

Everlastings, Pussy-Toes
Antennaria spp.

These small composites (several species occur on the arctic coast) consist of an inflorescence of one to several heads, supported on a central scape, which bears a few narrow stem leaves. A basal rosette of somewhat lanceolate or spatulate leaves, usually less than 1.5 cm in length, is usually covered with a grey woolly or silky pubescence, which looks just like a furry coating.

This "furriness" is common in plants that occur at high altitudes where there is little atmospheric protection from the sun's radiation. In his excellent little book, *Arctic Adaptations in Flowering Plants*, D. Savile (1972) states, "I suspect that most of the arctic plants that are densely pubescent throughout, such as *Antennaria* spp., have been derived fairly recently and with little genetic change from alpine regions."

The common names of this plant are European in origin, and refer ("everlasting") to the fact that the foliage and dried seedhead of this plant persists well into the winter, without appearing to brown or change at all. The name "pussy-toes" comes from the fact that the flowers and developing seedhead resemble the furry paws of a small cat.

Everlastings, Pussy-Toes Hapkoak mikan maklongayut, hongayaktonlo naotiat avangni Englanmi naoyokton, imaton taiyaoyukton "pussy toes," imaton pussikiaton etigaiton inamik.

Alpine Arnica, Alpine Daisy
Arnica alpina

This bold yellow composite is really characteristic of late summer in the central arctic. It is a fairly large plant, growing to 20-30 cm in height, and the flowerheads are 3.5-5 cm across. This species usually bears only a single erect sunflower-like head, but occasionally two are present, on the same scape. Both ray and disk flowers are a strong bright yellow. The leaves are opposite, almost sessile, narrow and straplike. There may be a basal rosette of leaves.

Another species of *Arnica* occurs along the coast as far east as Coppermine and the mouth of the Hood River. This is *A. louiseana*, which can be distinguished from *A. alpina* mainly by the fact that the flowerhead is nodding rather than erect. *A. louiseana* also has wider, slightly toothed leaves with short, winged petioles.

Everlastings
Antennaria / Sam Kapolak

Alpine Arnica *Arnica alpina* / Sam Kapolak

Arnica alpina

Arnica is widely used by herbalists as a poultice for the treatment of sprains, strains, and bruises. It should *never* be taken internally, as it affects the heart, and can cause digestive upsets. It is not used by the Inuit in our area.

Alpine Daisy, Arnica Angiug ona kogitak naotiat, naoyuktok hitkokit tikiplogin, nunaptini naoyukton koyaginak. Imaiton kogitan naotian amigaiton allatkiktakton. Ona kinigoni naotiat, ehiviotaijavantin naotiagik, naotiagik naloamayut napavini.

Hapkoat naotiat atoktaoginakton havaotigiblogik kangagalok. Paotongoyagangat, angnigangalonit teliuhogit hapkoat havaotigiyutait, mamingnagiyukton. Ona teliutat, niukagoalogo. Tokonaknaktot.

Aster
Aster spp.

Asters look like small daisies (10 - 20 cm) with narrow ray flowers. In our area, they are bluish violet with yellow disk flowers. The aster group is a large and complex one, but it is a group characteristic of the south. Not many species occur in our area.

The pygmy aster, the only aster found on the arctic islands, also occurs on the mainland, but is endemic to the western central arctic. The similar Siberian aster occurs on the mainland, not on the islands, and has a much wider distribution, through Alaska and the western arctic. *Aster sibiricus* has serrate margins on its narrow leaves, while *A. pygmaeus* has slightly broader leaves, with entire margins (no notches or serrations). There can be overlaps in these leaf shapes, and the serrations can be very small, so these two species are difficult to distinguish, especially from photographs. When shooting pictures, be sure to photograph a leaf, close-up, so you can later identify the plant.

Asters Hapkoat mikait naotiat toatunik naotialik. Hilata naotiap papogayut, kitkataot kogitaoyuk.

Arctic Daisy
Chrysanthemum integrifolium

It's not like the chrysanthemums used as house plants, or at football games, but this little plant is quite attractive. It blooms late in the summer, after many other species are finished, so is relatively conspicuous. The flowerhead of *Chrysanthemum integrifolium* resembles that of the wild chamomile (*Matricaria ambigua*), but the plant is much smaller (about 10 - 15 cm high), and the leaves are basal and linear, instead of being finely divided as are those of *Matricaria*.

The arctic daisy usually occurs in well-drained areas, often on gravelly tundra or old strandlines. It seldom grows on sea beaches, or in areas exposed to salt spray.

Aster *Aster sibericus*

Arctic Daisy
Chrysanthemum integrifolium

Chrysanthemum arcticum is similar and occurs on the Alaskan coast, in the Mackenzie delta, and around Hudson Bay, but not on the arctic islands. Its flowerhead is much the same, but the leaves are wedge-shaped, and lack hairs. It is generally taller, 15 - 25 cm high.

The chrysanthemums and their relatives have been put to a fascinating commercial use. They (especially the genus *Pyrethrum*) are grown commercially, mostly in Africa, to produce pyrethrins, used as insecticides. Pyrethrins are chemicals produced within the plant to discourage insect feeding. They can be extracted and used in sprays and other formulations to kill insects. They are considered very "safe" insecticides because they are not long-lived, and do not accumulate in the food chain.

Arctic Daisy, Chrysanthemum Ona mikak naotiat naoyoktok avalitomik, amigaiyuktoklonit paniumanikmi nunami. Hilata naotiat kakotak, kitkataot kogiktat. Hapkoat ajikotagiyukita angitkia naotiat, atongaoyait kehemi kopihimaiton allat naotiaton.

Fleabane
Erigeron sp.

The fleabanes are relatively early-flowering composites with narrow white (in our area) ray flowers and yellow disk flowers that contain both stamens and pistils. The stems of most local species are covered with translucent hairs, producing sort of a miniature "greenhouse effect", allowing the sun's radiation to penetrate, but then preventing the loss of heat through air circulation against the surface of the plant.

There are four to seven fleabanes that can occur along the arctic coast. These are tough to identify, as the diagnostic characteristics are mostly microscopic. The only easy one is *E. compositus*, which has lobed or "dissected" (divided) leaves. All the rest have straplike leaves. Use the keys in Porsild and Cody (1980) to identify the species along the coast. Only three species, *E. compositus*, *E. humilis*, and *E. eriocephalus*, occur on Banks and Victoria Islands.

E. humilis is probably the most common in our area; growing in moist grassy places, often below late snowbanks. The involucral bracts in this species appear bluish-black — the crosswalls in the hairs on the dense hairs are purplish. Get out your hand-lens!

Sea-Shore Chamomile
Matricaria ambigua

This plant fits the image of "daisy" — it is pure white with a yellow centre, it produces one to several flowerheads per plant, and is graceful and obvious, everything a daisy "ought to be."

The sea-shore chamomile also obligingly grows along the sea-shore, in fairly stable sandy areas, often in association with *Equisetum*, *Lathyrus* (beach-pea), or sedges.

Fleabane *Erigeron humilis*

Erigeron humilis / Sam Kapolak

Sea-shore Chamomile
Matricaria ambigua / Sam Kapolak

According to Schofield (1989) the name "Matricaria" is derived from the Latin roots *matrix* ("mother") and *caria* ("dear"). This refers to the long historical use of this genus as medicine for female problems and as a medicine for children. Flowerheads of the closely-related pineapple weed (*Matricaria matricarioides*) are widely used as a relaxing tea and medicine, by the Dene, Aleuts, and herbalists everywhere. It is said to be an effective insect repellent and to remove fish odors from your hands. This introduced weed smells strongly of pineapple when crushed, and was used as a "strewing herb" in the Middle Ages.

Wild Chamomile Ona naotiat ijukitok mikanmit, hilata kakotak, kitkataot kogitak. Atongaoyait piniktomik kupihimayun, atongaoyaitontaok allat.

Imaton atiktoahimayuk Matricaria, ima okatan mamam nakogiyain. Ingilganit havoatoayukton teliuhogo, ologaiholiganga aonaknikmin, Nutagangnoanot atoyutait kaotaligangamik, kegotiniligangamiklo. Humanikmiut naotiat ajikotagiyukitait.

Wormwood
Artemisia tilesii

This plant is familiar to most people who live on the mainland in the central arctic. It is a relatively large plant, and grows where the soil has been disturbed, especially around camps, animal burrows, and airstrips. It doesn't produce beautiful flowers, and isn't "showy". When you crush a leaf, it produces a lovely aromatic smell. This smell comes from an oil in the plant, called "absinthol".

Artemisia flowers are yellowish green, with thin ray flowers that never open out flat, and yellowish disk flowers generally hidden by the ray flowers. The large, palmately lobed leaves are about 10 cm in diameter.

Wormwood is an herb that has been used throughout history; its use is recorded in Egyptian scrolls from 1600 B.C. It got its name, "wormwood" from the fact that it was used to kill some kinds of intestinal worms. Northern people (especially the Yupik and Inupiat of Alaska) use poultices of wormwood for aching muscles and minor wounds, sore gums, and swollen hands and feet (Schofield, 1989). Many books on herbal medicine provide dozens of other uses. Though wormwood can be useful as a medicine, you should be careful about eating it or drinking tea made from this plant. In large quantities, it can cause coma and convulsions.

When you are breaking camp and packing up your tent, roll a few wormwood leaves in the tent. This will make the tent smell fresh and clean.

Although *A. tilesii* is very obvious and common on the mainland, it is not common on the arctic islands. There are several other species of *Artemisia* that occur in the central arctic. These are much smaller plants, not necessarily associated with human habitations, and not necessarily aromatic. *Artemisia borealis* is fairly common on sandy delta soils at Bathurst Inlet, and *A. richardsoniana* and *A. hyperborea* are more

Matricaria ambigua

Wormwood *Artemisia tilesii*

Artemisia borealis

common on Victoria Island and Banks Island. Use Porsild and Cody (1980) to identify these small plants, as they are very similar.

Wormwood, Artemisia Hapkoat atongaoyat ilihimayaoyut koyaginak nunami hamani Central Arcticmi. Naoyokton initoklini, hogaklo hitaini, milviknilo. Pinihitiyuitok naotiaginik, naotiakokitok. Mamahitiyuktok atongaoya pilokligangat. Tipa atongaoyam ohoani mamahitivaton ima taivaktan "absinthol."

Ona atotaoyuktok atongaoyak taimagalok. Atoknin tetegaktaohimayuk Egypmiuni, Imaton 3,591 okioni atotaogakpakton.

Atilik imaton keyop kopilgoa, ingaloat kopilgonikangata atoyukaloagamigit. Inuit koyaginak, Inupiat kehemi atoyuktait aniknaligangamik, kilinoanilo, kanikmotlo, bovigangata algait etigaitlo havaotigiyuktait.

Oalaligangavit tamayaiyagangavit, tupik ominga atongaoyamik imokahiujavat, mamahitiyuktok tupikmik.

Makpigani tetegataohimayun kangnot hapkoat atongaoyat atulikpagait. Ona havaotaogaloahoni, negeyuhaongitot, niukagoilogo. Negevalagoni ona ihomaiknaktok, kekelakinaktoklo.

 # Coltsfoot
Petasites sagittatus

This is one of the largest herbaceous plants in our area — the leaves can be up to 30 cm long, but commonly average around 15 - 20 cm in length and 10 - 15 cm wide. The oblong arrowhead-shaped leaves remind one of plants found far to the south; they are almost tropical in appearance. The specific name of this plant refers to the arrowhead shape of the leaves, from the Latin term *sagitta*, meaning "an arrow".

The coltsfoot has many flowerheads, arranged in a tight raceme on a thick, fleshy stem. These have white ray flowers, and are fragrant, though the odor can be somewhat overpowering. This plant blooms early in the summer, in mid-June on the coast, before the leaves appear. It is visited by many bumblebees at this time, and probably is an early source of nectar during a time when few other plants are blooming. In our area, it is not common, but is so striking that it has been included.

The leaves of coltsfoot have been long used by herbalists to make a cough syrup, which is often flavored by honey. It is said to relieve persistent coughs, bronchial congestion, and asthma. I can find no evidence that the Inuit of the central arctic used it, although Schofield (1989) and Heller (1985) mention that the leaves and flowering stems were used as a food in Alaska and Siberia, by local Eskimo groups.

There are two species in our area; *P. sagittatus* is a mainland boreal forest/low arctic species, which doesn't extend onto the arctic islands. *P. frigidus* is circumpolar, in our area extending from Alaska and the Yukon across the coast and onto Banks, Vistoria and the western Parry Islands. It can be distinguished from *P. sagittatus* by its smaller, triangular leaves. The leaves of *P. frigidus* are about the size of the track of a caribou calf

Coltsfoot *Petasites sagittatus*

Petasites sagittatus

Petasites sagittatus / Sam Kapolak

(4 - 6 cm), while those of *P. sagittatus* are the size of the track of a young caribou cow (10 - 15 cm) in our area (they can be much larger in the south — up to 30 cm).

Coltsfoot Ona atongaoyak angiyuk naoyoktok haniani initoklini, kinipanikmi. Naotiaga naotgayoktok atongaoyainit, naotiagit kangani naotiagiaton. Atongaoyait angiyun, ilani algat ajikotagiyuktait. Hapkoat ahini naoyuhaton itot hamaniungiktok. Atongaoyait hongayakton kangani, ataitaok kakotan kalikokton.

Dwarf Hawksbeard, Alpine Hawksbeard
Crepis nana

This unusual and unique little plant can't be mistaken for anything else. It is a tiny composite, no more than 1.5 cm high, and often less than 5 cm across. It forms a flat basal rosette of spoon-shaped leaves with a purplish tint, and the small flowerheads barely extend above the leaves.

This plant has a wide range. I have found it on high passes in Denali National Park in Alaska, and it occurs in central and eastern Asia as well. In our area, it clings to the windswept and spray-lashed beaches of algal limestone islands, and grows on gravel bars in the mouths of arctic rivers, subject to annual flooding. With its yellow flowers spread out like a tiny bracelet at the edge of the rosette, it is truly a miracle of adaptation and resilience. The habit of blooming while the flowerheads still touch the rosette is an adaptation to keep the developing ovaries within the warmest stratum of air, close to the ground and the sun-warmed rocks (Savile, 1972).

Fireworks Flower
Saussurea angustifolia

This is a cheery little composite, whose purple pistils tipped with white seem to explode like miniature fireworks in the tundra. Three to five discoid flowerheads are arranged in a corymb, or tight, round-topped inflorescence.

The stem is dark purplish-green, and the leaves are narrow and straplike. The basal leaves have distinct petioles, but the stem ones do not. The fireworks flower is small, rarely more than 15 - 20 cm in our area.

The genus *Saussurea* is an Asiatic one, with only a few species in western North America. *S. angustifolia* has a limited distribution, from northeastern Asia across the Bering Straits and into the central arctic, where it occurs as far east as the Melville Peninsula and the northwestern coast of Hudson Bay. It is one of the last plants to bloom in the summer. The seedheads, with their cream-colored pappus bristles, persist into the following year. With your hand lens, take a look at the tawny pappus bristles — they are featherlike (plumose), and quite lovely.

Dwarf Hawksbeard *Crepis nana*/Sam Kapolak

Fireworks Flower
Saussurea angustifolia
David Middleton

Fireworks Flower, Saussurea Papogayuk ona naotiat, naotiayoktok aoyakhimahagangami. Naotiagit kagaktitaotiton iliyukton, kagakhimayuton.

GROUNDSELS · RAGWORTS

The genus *Senecio* is a large one, world-wide in distribution, with a lot of variety. The name, "senecio" comes from the Latin *senes* ("old man"), and refers to the white pappus bristles (bristles at the tip of the ovaries). Some senecios in tropical areas reach the size of small trees. In our area, there are probably about four species.

The leaves of *Senecio*.are always alternate, unlike those of *Arnica*, which are opposite. This makes identification a little easier.

Groundsel
Senecio atropurpureus

This is an interesting little composite — in our area, it appears in two forms, one with both disk and ray (ligulate) flowers, and one that lacks the ray flowers, and looks completely different.

The disk flowers (and ray flowers, if present) are a bright yellow with a hint of orange, arranged in a tight head. In the central arctic, the flowerheads without ray flowers are most common. A single flowerhead is borne on a slender stem, which may have four to six sessile, somewhat fleshy leaves. It also has a basal rosette of ovate, petiolate leaves, which are 1 - 2 cm long.

Senecio atropurpureus has a scattered growth habit, and seems to prefer heath tundra that is neither too wet nor too dry, protected areas where snow likely collects fairly early in the winter.

Senecio, Groundsel Okoat aglingnakton malgonik allatkinik naoyokton, hilatilingmik, hilataitomiklo. Ajikotagiyait allat naotiat, ajikingitot kehemi. Ona ajikotagiukita alla naotiat, atongaoyait allangayut kehemi. Napaviani atongaoyain aipaitonik naoyokton, katimangitomik naotiyokton. Makpigani naonaitkotait kiniklogit haffoma naotiat atongaoyait.

Black-Tipped Groundsel
Senecio lugens

This little groundsel (5 - 20 cm) has several (3 - 12) flowerheads in a loose terminal corymb, several stem leaves, and basal leaves with distinct petioles. Each flowerhead has both ray and disk flowers; these are bright yellow. The lower stem leaves and basal leaves are finely-toothed. This species can be distinguished from other groundsels in the area by the black tips on its involucral bracts.

Groundsel *Senecio atropurpureus*

Senecio atropurpureus

Black-tipped Groundsel
Senecio lugens / J. Irons

This species was described by John Richardson, surgeon-naturalist with the Franklin expedition. He first collected it at Bloody Fall on the Coppermine River. Porsild and Cody (1980) describe its naming: "The black tips of the involucral bracts inspired the specific name, from the Latin *lugeo* (to mourn), and refers to the massacre at Bloody Fall on the Coppermine River, of a group of unsuspecting Eskimo, by the Indian warriors who, in 1771, accompanied Samuel Hearne." John Richardson's journal (*Arctic Ordeal*, ed. by C. Stuart Houston, 1985) poignantly expresses his sympathy for the fear shown by the Inuit his party encountered near Bloody Fall — it is easy to imagine that this concern carried over into his scientific description of this plant.

 ## Mastodon Flower
Senecio congestus

A relatively large and coarse plant for the central arctic, the mastodon flower can reach a meter in height, though it is usually smaller. Its yellow flowerheads are borne in tight, woolly clusters, one terminal and the rest on lateral branches arising from the stem or the base of the plant. The stem is brownish, hairy, about 1 cm in diameter, and hollow.

The leaves of this species are sessile on the stem, and linear, with shallow teeth.

In the early stages of growth, the leaves, stem, and closed flowerheads are all covered with translucent hairs — producing a "greenhouse effect" close to the surface of the plant, essentially extending the growing season by a few vital days by allowing the sun to warm the tissues, and preventing the heat from escaping.

According to Porsild and Cody (1980), *S. congestus* "is hapaxanthic or once-flowering, dying completely after having flowered and produced seeds, but in the high latitudes, specimens in which the flowers of the year were killed by early frost, may flower and fruit the following year." This is probably the largest annual in our area — it is amazing that a plant can produce this much mass, and flower and set seed in a single season, which extends from mid-June to late August at the most.

 ## Dandelion
Taraxacum spp.

To visitors from the south, it is always a surprise, tinged with either delight or disappointment, to find dandelions in their wanderings in the arctic. These are such familiar plants in southern lawns, that people just do not expect to find them here. Only one species (*Taraxacum officinale*) found in the N.W.T. is an alien, and it has not yet found its way to the arctic coast. The dandelion group is a large and complex one, with numerous representatives in alpine areas in Europe and across North America. The common name, "dandelion", comes from the French *dente*

Mastodon Flower
Senecio congestus / Pat Thagard

Senecio congestus / J. Irons

de lion, which refers to the toothed leaves; it means "tooth of the lion."

The genus *Taraxacum* is relatively easy to recognize (although it can be confused with the goatsbeards, hawkweeds, and hawksbeards). The flowerheads have only ray flowers (ligulate flowers), and lack disk flowers. They have single flowerheads, borne on a hollow, leafless scape, a basal rosette of toothed leaves, and bitter, milky sap. Most are yellow, but a few are white, some tinged with purple. They have stout taproots that anchor the plant securely in the ground. They are hardy perennials, dying back to the taproot and "crown" at the centre of the basal rosette in winter, and thrusting forth new leaves and flowers in the spring.

According to Porsild and Cody (1980), many *Taraxacum* species do not produce fertile pollen, but produce their seeds by parthenogenesis (without fertilization). By this mechanism, which does not involve the exchange of genetic material between two plants, minor variations tend to persist, making identification even more difficult.

Most (but not all) of the dandelions along the arctic coast are associated with soil that has been enriched by nesting birds, burrowing mammals, or humans. They are common on bird nesting islands, but, even there, they tend to become established at the edge of traditional nests, where the incubating bird defecates over the edge of the nest. They also become established below traditional raptor nest sites on cliffs. And, we find them on Inuit campsites. They are not common on those that were used years ago, but are not being used now. We find them on sites that are still being used, at least intermittently.

The dandelions are a complex group, and are difficult to identify, requiring a relatively specialized terminology. The keys in Porsild and Cody (1980) are quite good, so we will refer the reader to those. A surprising number of species occur on the arctic islands, so one would need to use the keys (and distribution maps) for any that are found in our area.

Dandelions are used throughout the world as a food plant — new spring leaves are used in salads and boiled as a pot-herb, flowers can be used to make jelly, and the roots boiled, baked, used in soups, or roasted and ground to make a coffee substitute (Walker, 1984). They are used in innumerable ways as medicine, and their sticky sap has been used to cure warts. In Russia during World War II, a dandelion species was cultivated as a commercial source of latex for rubber (Schofield, 1989). There is no record that they were used by the Inuit, however.

Dandelion Ona atia dandelion, frenchmiutanit atikhimayun, ima okahotik kegotakton laiyaton, hapkoat kegotiton hina atongaoyap inamik. Hapkoat atongaoyat koyaginak naotiyukton tahamani kehemi ivikni naitoni iglukavini. Nunaptini naotiayuiton, naoyukton initokliminikni, hogatlo kopanoatlo anakataniani. Naoyokton kopanoat ivavingni kikitani, oblonilo hogatlo hitaini.

Hapkoat nunaptini naotiayuinakmik atotiayuitavot, ahinit nunami kehemi koyaginak atoktaoyuktok ona atongaoyak. Atongaoyait egablogit negeyuktait, naotiangit imiuyuktait, napavitaot naotivinlo nekilialiuyuktait, ilangitaot havaotigiblogit.

Dandelion *Taraxacum*, at gull nests

Taraxacum / Sam Kapolak

Taraxacum, seedheads

Bathurst Inlet / Bob Poffenroth

Botanizing in the Arctic Coast Communities

- Holman
- Coppermine
- Bathurst Inlet
- Cambridge Bay
- Gjoa Haven
- Spence Bay
- Pelly Bay

Communities of the Arctic Coast

The arctic coast region of the Northwest Territories is truly remote wilderness, visited by only a few outsiders. Yet, throughout this area are scattered a number of small communities, each in its own way a centre of activity, and home to a few hundred people.

All the arctic coast region was under the ice of the great continental glaciers as recently as 6000-8000 years ago. After the retreat of the Wisconsin Glacier, a thin file of people came into the area from the west, across the Bering Straits, along the Alaskan and Yukon coasts, and into the central arctic. They wandered this cold northern land, living off the bounty of the sea and of the land, the caribou, musk oxen, seal, whales, fish, and other animals. These people were the ancestors of many of the Inuit residents of today's arctic coast communities.

From the east came the early European explorers, searching for mineral wealth and for a passage to the rich Indies, and later, hunting the whales that roamed these icy seas. More Europeans came, to reap a rich harvest of fur, or to trade with the Inuit, encouraging them to trap white foxes and wolverines. They were followed by the missionaries, who established small churches in the embryonic communities springing up around the trading posts. The Royal Northwest Mounted Police came to act as the representative of the faraway government in Ottawa, and to uphold the law at the edge of the known world. In the last fifty years, mineral exploration, the Distant Early Warning Line/North Warning System, government services, and air transportation entered the northern picture, and now the arctic coast is dotted with small communities.

Each community is a mixture of native people who have come in off the land, and kablunak (white) people who are in the arctic for a variety of reasons. The fur trade has shrunk, mining of the mineral wealth is incredibly expensive, and people no longer want to live the hard nomadic life led by their parents and grandparents. Though promising advances are being made in the area of fisheries, in the production of art and craft objects for sale, and in the commercial sale of musk ox and caribou meat, tourism is becoming more and more important to these small communities.

Most of the central arctic is a real frontier of tourism. This has its negatives and positives — it is expensive to travel there, and services may not be up to the standards of the Riviera. On the other hand, the visitor to the area is far more likely to see life as it was, and to get to know the local people on a personal basis. And then, there is the land, untamed, immense and ancient, dwarfing Man and his communities. No matter how you travel across the face of the land or of the sea, you are sharply aware of the powerful forces that control all life here at the edge.

Botanizing in the Communities

Visitors interested in plants as part of their northern experience will experience the frontier — you will encounter an incredibly rich flora, with the blooming season crammed into a few short weeks, and virtually nobody to interpret it for you! Plants were not an important part of the Inuit way of life on the arctic coast, and most of the kablunak people in these communities are just beginning to develop an interest. There are no garden clubs or museum groups to sustain interest, and few environmental interpreters, though that is changing. There are just plants, millions of them, blooming frantically, carpeting the ground.

Expect some "do-it-yourself" botanizing, and expect some pretty surprising discoveries.

Here's a suggestion that has worked for me. Pay close attention from the air when you are flying into a community, looking around the margins of the community. You are looking for different habitats — for tundra ponds surrounded by interesting meadows, for isolated spots of greenery high on rocky ridges, for little waterfalls and small streams with streambank communities at their edges, for eskers or gravelly drumlins, and for wide sweeps of vegetated tundra. Use the airport, the sea, and the town as reference points, and you'll be better prepared to find your special spots later.

Once you are in the community, check at the hamlet office (and perhaps with the Renewable Resources officer) for the names of people in the community who are interested in the flowers. (In Cambridge Bay, check with the Arctic Coast Tourist Association in the Kitikmeot Regional Visitor's Centre.) Everyone knows everyone else in these small communities, and will be glad to guide you to someone with similar interests. If that person is in town, he/she will probably welcome a fellow botanizer, and can guide you to the prime spots. This book may or may not be available in the community, it might be thoughtful to take an extra copy for a local person who spends time in the field with you, as field guides to this area are just not available.

When walking, looking for flowers, check out likely habitats with binoculars, or by walking to the site and looking it over carefully. Many arctic plants are so small that their flowers simply do not show up from a distance. You must get close to find them. Even a few steps can make a tremendous difference.

As a visitor, either do not collect, or be extremely conservative in your collecting, and *do not collect* any plant that seems rare in the area.

Few arctic plants will do well when transplanted to the south. Some plants do all right when grown from seeds, but remember that, for the most part, you are on a frontier for flowers as well as for people. The reproductive systems are working for these plants, but they are struggling to live in an inhospitable environment. Not many people visit, but those who do should respect the plant inhabitants as well as the human and animal inhabitants of these areas.

Sources of Information

I have relied on several people for information about the communities and their flora. Based upon his years of experience in northern service with the R.C.M.P., Glenn Warner has been of great assistance in providing history and background. Retired Bishop of the Arctic, John Sperry spent thirty years in the arctic and has been particularly helpful in providing information on the communities of the central arctic.

Joanne Irons and Pat Thagard, residents of their respective communities, wrote the sections on Coppermine and Cambridge Bay, and they have done an admirable job. I have interviewed people in other communities and have used plant records in the literature to develop what I hope is an adequate floral picture of the area. Take it with a grain of salt, and enjoy discovering the plant communities for yourself!

The Northwest Territories Data Book published by Outcrop is a valuable source of information on communities in the N.W.T., as well as a wealth of other information. A tourism directory published by the Government of the Northwest Territories contains information on accommodations, services, and guide services. Brochures for each community, containing maps of the community and of the area are available from Arctic Coast Tourist Association, P.O. Box 91, Cambridge Bay, N.W.T. X0E 0C0, phone (403) 983-2224.

Pat Thagard

Holman (Uluqsaqtuuq)

The late spring sun illuminates the steep south-facing cliffs above the settlement of Holman, shrinking the snow patches and warming the rocks. Amid the snow and on the talus slopes and clifftops, the purple mountain saxifrage bursts into riotous bloom. It will soon be followed by many other species, on the slopes, on the rocky tundra, along streams, and at the edges of the small lakes, until the tundra is a kaleidoscope of color and pattern — the deep blue of *Oxytropis arctobia*, and the creamy white of the mountain avens, the magenta of the rhododendron along the edges of small streams, and the yellow of arctic poppy and pink of alpine azalea on the gravelly uplands and the rocky edges of the lakes.

Holman is located on the southwestern tip of the Diamond Jenness Peninsula on the western side of Victoria Island, north of Prince Albert Sound and south of Minto Inlet. Facing Amundsen Gulf and backed by massive escarpments, it is situated on three bays, which provides a scenic variety of habitats for plants.

In 1940, a Hudson's Bay post and Roman Catholic mission were built, serving an economy based on white fox trapping and seal hunting. Until 1962, when the Anglican mission was established, missionaries travelled to the community from Coppermine. Now, approximately 400 people live in this small community. Fortunately (in view of the decline of the fur industry as a basis of economic support), a thriving arts and crafts industry developed when Father Henry Tardi introduced silkscreen printmaking to the community in 1940, and has continued to expand. Helen Kalvak, and, more recently, Mary Okeena, have astounded the art world with their exquisite prints. Some of the women create lovely sealskin or handsewn parkas, dolls, silkscreen hangings, table linen, and hand silkscreened cards.

The area is part of the ancestral home of the Copper Inuit; who provided assistance to Vilhjalmar Steffansson on his Canadian Arctic Expedition in 1911. Today, some people guide sporthunters on polar bear or musk ox hunts; others produce artwork for the Holman Eskimo Co-operative, and still others still trap or live in the traditional way, fishing and hunting caribou, musk ox, or seal. Ecotourism is becoming more important to this area, and naturalist expeditions, led by the local people, add another facet to the local economy.

The flower season is very short here, essentially the first three weeks of July. All the bloom is crammed into this short season, with spectacular results. If you visit Holman at this time, you'll find wildflowers all around the town, and especially rich shows of flowers along the road to Okpilik (Ukpillik) and Air Force Lakes, near all three bays, and on the cliffs to the east of the community. One of the most uncommon flowers in our area is fairly easy to find here — it is the rock-jasmine (*Androsace chamaejasme*), a beautiful and fragrant white flower with a yellow "eye", which can form mats over the rocky surface. A local grove of willow "trees" has achieved a certain amount of local notariety, as it has developed far north of most other "tall" willows. The trees here are all of 60 cm tall! Winnie Joss remembers visiting these willows as a child, and thinking of them as big trees. There are other prostrate willows, but far fewer than on the mainland. Arctic cotton forms great drifts at the edges of the little tundra ponds. The arctic lupine is present, but far smaller than on the mainland, and quite localized. The white arctic heather is used by the local people as a fuel for boiling tea, as it burns readily even when green.

My grateful thanks to Winnie Joss, Jeff Dixon, and Marci Chesterfield for information on the area and the flowers. Marci Chesterfield puts it well, "The summer is so short, but it is very beautiful, especially when you know there's ten months of the year when you will not see the plants at all! And remember, it can snow on you at any time, while you're looking at the flowers!"

J. Irons

Coppermine (Kulgluktuk) *by Joanne Irons*

West of the mouth of the Coppermine River, Coppermine faces a panoramic view of the Coronation Gulf, its islands and sandbars. Steep cliffs, high ridges and rocky outcrops of diabase, shale, and dolomite provide a scenic backdrop for this hamlet of over 1000 people. Traditionally, this was a seasonal fishing and hunting camp for the nomadic Copper Inuit. The Hudson's Bay Company and the Anglican Church were established here in 1928, at the community known as "Fort Hearne". The R.C.M.P. post was called the "Coppermine River Post".

Strangely enough, a real copper mine has never operated here. The community takes its name from the river that flows 845 km through the Barrenlands to the Coronation Gulf, between Bathurst Inlet and Great Bear Lake. It was named by Moses Norton, Governor of Fort Prince of Wales. On November 6, 1769, Norton dispatched Samuel Hearne to "the Copper Mine River" to locate the source of copper that the northern Indians were bringing to the fort (on Hudson Bay, near the present site of Churchill). The local Inuit placename for the river and the community is "Kugluktuk", meaning "where the water falls", referring to the rapids on the river. The Coppermine River is an important canoeing and rafting river, enticing because of its wildlife, scenery, and the fact that it runs to the Arctic Ocean through some of the wildest country left on earth.

Samuel Hearne never found the great copper mines (although he gathered some interesting legends about disappearing copper mines), and his first encounter with the Inuit ended tragically. Hearne's guide, Matonabbee and his warriors, on July 17, 1771, attacked an Inuit fishing camp by the rapids, and massacred the inhabitants. Hearne, a stunned bystander to the slaughter, named the spot "Bloody Fall".

The floral display in the Coppermine area peaks during the last week of June and the first two weeks of July in most years. The roadside, the beach and duck ponds, the tundra meadows, and the cliffs offer four distinctly different wildflower habitats within easy walking distance. When hiking in the area, it is advisable to wear rubber boots, as some areas are swampy.

The road leading to the edge of the river provides easy access to some plants that will grow in disturbed soil, as the gravelly road margins offer a foothold for yarrow, wormwood, wild chamomile, fireweed, several gentians, mustards, and wild dandelions. A few metres to the west of the road, you can find primrose (check for *Primula egaliksensis* along the river, and *P. stricta* along the seashore), and an uncommon small white willow herb, *Epilobium palustre*. This is the only place they're found around Coppermine.

Leave the road and hike toward the rocky outcrops of the Coppermine Cliffs. You will find heather, blueberry, cranberry, bearberry, and crowberries underfoot. At the rocks, it is easy to find mountain avens, moss campion, purple and prickly saxifrage. On the river side of the cliffs, warmed by the 24 hour summer sun, alpine arnica, pussy-toes, fleabane, and the bulblet saxifrage add their colors to this arctic bouquet. At the base of the cliffs, damp from snowmelt, you'll find Lapland rosebay, yellow marsh saxifrage, yellow water crowfoot, Richardson's anemone, few-flowered anemone (*Anemone parviflora*), Labrador tea, bog rosemary, black-tipped groundsel and a good display of golden saxifrage (*Chrysosplenium tetrandrum*), also called northern water carpet.

It's an easy hike over the tundra to the west side of Saddleback Hill. However, there are wet areas, with arctic cotton and mastodon flower, and you may have to do some hummock hopping if you've forgotten waterproof footwear. Butterwort, several louseworts, lupine, saussurea, shrubby cinquefoil, and several vetches inhabit these meadows. On the rocky outcrops facing the airport and the Coronation Gulf, some of the less common plants blossom — northern bog orchid, side-flowered wintergreen, large-flowered wintergreen, and the rare red-stemmed saxifrage.

Once you've made your way back to the ocean road, the picnic area is an excellent starting place for a beach walk. Here, arctic gentians (prob. *Gentiana propinqua*), and Siberian asters bloom in late summer, as well as grass-of-Parnassus, paintbrush, and chamomile. On the sandy beach, several species of *Oxytropis*, beach pea, and seabeach sandwort stretch out. By the duck ponds, you'll find marsh marigold and yellow water crowfoot, with fields of vetch, lupine, bladder campion, cinquefoil, and paintbrush flourishing beyond the ponds. Still farther down, beyond the barge marker, you'll delight in a rare find, a stand of blue and white flax.

If your time permits, travel to the end of the new dump road, and veer west to the Honda trail to arrive at Heart Lake. The wide sandy beach offers the only spot around with pure white river beauties (*Epilobium latifolium*). West of the cliffs, there's a huge stand of mastodon flowers, and large willows occupy the far shore.

If you are canoeing the Coppermine, or take an overnight hike to Bloody Fall, just above the eagle's nests, on the west side of the river, you will encounter a splendid stand of wild chives. The black-tipped groundsel grows on the grassy slopes — this is the "type locality" for this species, likely the population from which Richardson described the species.

Time permitting, consider a trip to the Rae River, where offerings include bluebells (*Campanula* spp.) and star gentian (*Lomatogonium rotatum*) on the grassy plains, and fragrant rock-jasmine on the cliffs. Or, consider a trip to the islands or Mackenzie Point to experience more of Coppermine's vibrant collection of wildflowers.

When in Coppermine, check with the Hamlet office for the names of people in town who are interested in wildflowers.

Bathurst Inlet (Kingoak) and Bay Chimo (Umingmaktok)

Immense sills of diabase bisect the dark waters of Bathurst Inlet, and the tundra sweeps away to the rounded edges of the downdrop block that formed this deep arm of the Coronation Gulf millions of years ago. The Burnside River tumbles over the edge of the Canadian Shield in a series of waterfalls in a deep gorge, then spreads out to create a meandering floodplain as it reaches the salt water. Outcrops of red quartzite and ancient algal limestone provide safe nesting havens for gulls and eider ducks, and numerous tundra ponds rimmed with arctic cotton reflect the azure of the sky. Due to the relief of the land, the complexity of its geology, the fertility of its soil, and the presence of many rivers (the Western, the Huikitak, the Gordon, and the Hood) and uncounted small streams, the Bathurst Inlet area harbors an incredible variety of plants.

There are two settlements on Bathurst Inlet, Bay Chimo (also known as Umingmaktok), and Bathurst Inlet (also called Kingoak).

Bay Chimo/Umingmaktok ("place of the musk ox") located on the northeast shore of the Inlet, is a small settlement of about 65 people, who largely depend on the land and waters of the inlet for their food. There is a short gravel runway, a small store, and one-room school (grades 1-3) taught by one of the local residents. There are no services for visitors in Bay Chimo.

Bathurst Inlet/Kingoak ("place below the 'Nose' Mountain, Kingaun") is located on the western shore of the Inlet, at the mouth of the Burnside

River, and is a tiny settlement of about 25 people. The residents live in the old ways during the winter, but are co-owners and co-operators in a world-famous naturalist lodge during the summer.

In the early 1900s, about 100 - 150 Inuit (of the ethnic group known as the Copper Eskimos) lived in the Bathurst Inlet area, travelling by kayak and on foot (assisted by a few sled dogs) depending primarily on the caribou for their sustenance, although they also hunted seal and fished for char, lake trout, and whitefish. The Hudson's Bay Company and the Canalaska Co. and independent traders such as Charles Klengenberg established trading posts in the area, and encouraged the development of a fur-based economy. In 1929, Dominion Explorers Ltd., a mineral exploration company, established a base camp on the Burnside delta. Their buildings were eventually moved a few hundred yards to the present site, and The Bay post was established in 1930. In 1935, the Burnside Mission was established by the Oblate order of the Roman Catholic Church. (*The Incredible Eskimo* was written by Fr. Raymond de Coccola, mission priest at Bathurst Inlet in the 1930s.) From 1955 to 1962, during the building of the DEW Line, Pacific Western Airlines operated a radio navigation beacon from the settlement.

Due to the general movement of people off the land and away from the traditional way of life in the 1960s, The Bay closed the post in 1964, moving it to Bay Chimo. The abandoned buildings were bought by Trish and Glenn Warner and partners Lyle Hawkins and Fred Ross, and Bathurst Inlet Lodge was started. The Lodge was one of the first to focus on natural history/history/geology/ traditional lifestyles, now popular as "ecotourism". In 1984, the Inuit joined the operation as partners in a unique venture - a small traditional community offering professional visitor services. There are no scheduled air services to the community, and no government services. The Lodge maintains a private airstrip, and provides summer services to the community. There is no lodging other than the very comfortable, but seasonal, accommodations provided by Bathurst Inlet Lodge. The Lodge also offers canoe outfitting services on three rivers in the area, the Mara, the Burnside, and the Hood.

Lodge programs introduce visitors to the natural and cultural history of the area. The use of a large pontoon boat enables visitors to see much of the middle third of the Inlet, and, short hiking trails around the Lodge enable guests to explore plant communities that range from a seashore community with marsh five-finger, seaside cinquefoil, several gentians, wild chamomile, seabeach sandwort, and beach pea to tundra ponds encircled by arctic cotton (*Eriophorum angustifolium*) and spangled with mare's tail. The Burnside delta provides excellent hiking, and intriguing botanizing — Sudetan lousewort is common, as is bog rosemary, grass-of-parnassus, thickets of willow and alder, several cinquefoils, and whole beaches covered with beach pea (*Lathyrus japonicus*).

Heath tundra surrounds the settlement, and the casual stroller will find an incredible tapestry of lapland rosebay, white arctic heather, lupine, five louseworts, paintbrush, bearberry, and lingonberry. The lodge staff sets up a wildflower trail each summer, with labels, and maintains labelled collections of fresh specimens to refresh memories after a day of exposure to dozens of new species.

Boat trips on the Inlet allow the visitor to see more plant communities, from musk ox meadows covered with rhododendron to marshes where yellow marsh saxifrage, bistort, purple bladder campion, *Cardamine pratensis*, marsh marigold, and arctic cotton dazzle the plant enthusiast. Hikes into the hills reveal more louseworts, purple and yellow mountain saxifrage, butterwort, alpine arnica, more heath tundra, and acres of mountain avens, spangled with woolly lousewort, harebells, dwarf fireweed, and clumps of arctic lupine.

The high rocky ridges support colorful lichen communities, and hardy species such as the purple mountain saxifrage, *Diapensia*, moss-campion, and alpine azalea. At the retreating edges of snowbanks, one can find the few-flowered anemone, Richardson's anemone, pygmy buttercups, a dwarf willow (*Salix herbacea*), and others. Finally, the islands in the Inlet support nesting bird populations that enrich the soil, and create favorable habitat for plants such as dandelions, the brook saxifrage, prickly saxifrage, mouse-eared chickweed, star chickweed, seaside bluebells, white bladder campion, several mustards, several cinquefoils, scurvy-grass, arctic poppies, and the striking Pallas' wallflower.

It is undoubtedly the generous mixture of habitats, and the protected nature of Bathurst Inlet that allows plant communities to exist in such profusion. It is truly an oasis in every sense of the word. The presence of a naturalist's lodge in the midst of all this diversity assures the visitor of good records and assistance with plant identifications.

Clayton Roberts

Cambridge Bay (Ikaluktutiak) *by Pat Thagard*

Cambridge Bay is located on the southeast side of Victoria Island, on a two-armed bay bearing the same name. This bay is a well-sheltered inlet off the Dease Strait just east of Long Point. This community of 1000 is located on the northwest side of the bay, to the southwest of Grenier Lake and Mount Pelly.

Scenic Mount Pelly beckons the visitor with a deceptive promise of only a short trip to provide a wide panorama from its highest point of approximately 690 ft. above sea level. Don't let it fool you, though! The lack of markers like trees and buildings make things seem closer than they are. What looks like a 45 minute walk will slowly stretch into a three hour trudge across the tundra. If you have the time and a good, sturdy pair of waterproof hiking boots, the walk is a great way to see the flora and fauna of the area. Plan to spend some time at Mount Pelly to prepare for the return journey. Or, have someone drive you out, and walk back to town.

The people of Cambridge Bay wait for the coming of the warm weather like children await the arrival of Christmas. Next to the return of the sun after its six week holiday below the horizon in winter, nothing else compares to the coming of summer and its profusion of flora. Thanks to the 24-hour sunlight in June and July, the land becomes a carpet of plants bursting into bloom. Although Victoria Island lacks the large number of species found on the mainland, the sheer numbers of the species present on the island more than makes up for the lack of diversity. The Cambridge Bay area is also the summer home to a very special kind of "tourist" — it is inundated every summer by over 50 species of birds, courting, chasing, singing, preening, setting, hatching, and feeding young. Mix this with the flowers, and you have an exciting annual festival of life.

Traditionally, the Copper Inuit of Victoria Island and the neighboring mainland came to the Cambridge Bay area to fish and hunt in summer, building up their stores for the winter. The excellent fishing in the area earned it the name Ikaluktutiak, which means "the fair fishing place". The local Co-op harvests and processes arctic char for retail sale in its local store, and exports it for canning for sale as a gourmet food item in the south. The ancestors of many current residents of Cambridge Bay have lived and hunted in the area for hundreds, if not thousands of years. One can still identify the remains of an ancient village just outside town on the road to Mount Pelly, and there are many caches along the river close to this ancient camping site. The native people of the area still retain many of their ties to the traditional way of life, but the town is currently the largest in the region, and the centre of government, communications, and transportation.

Cambridge Bay was named for the Duke of Cambridge, HRH Adolphus Fredrick, by Warren Dease and Thomas Simpson on their epic survey expeditions along the coast in 1837-1839. Some of the other explorers who sailed into Cambridge Bay include John Rae (in 1851) in search of the lost Franklin expedition, Richard Collinson (1852-1853), Roald Amundsen (1905) and Vilhjalmur Stefansson (1910).

The remains of the *Maud*, Roald Amundsen's three-masted schooner in which he traveled the Northwest Passage, can still be seen in the bay near the old stone church. The *Maud* was purchased by the H.B.C. in 1925, renamed the *Baymaud*, and used as a Hudson's Bay supply ship in the late 1920s. She transmitted the first arctic weather reports to the south in

1927. As the *Baymaud's* seaworthiness diminished, she was moored in the bay, and used as a floating warehouse. She developed a leak and sank in the shallows in 1932.

In the early 1920s, The Bay set up shop on the shores of Cambridge Bay. Some of the familiar red and white Bay buildings can still be seen near the newer Bay store now known as the Northern Store.

The churches built by both Anglican and Catholic missionaries in the 1920s are still standing, but only the Anglican church is still used today. An old stone church across the bay at the old town site is the former Roman Catholic mission. It was replaced by a newer building in the current town site.

The flowering season is very short on Victoria Island. Depending on the weather, plants can be in bloom as early as mid-June, but the floral season usually runs from the last week in June through the second week in August. Although the land seems covered with flowers, there are some places of special interest.

The road leading to Mount Pelly is a good place to start. You can stay on dry, even ground while hiking the road, and the disturbed soil at the sides of the road supports a diverse flora. Mats of mountain avens are everywhere, as well as several mustards, moss campion, a few low willows, several saxifrages, and several species of *Oxytropis*, especially the bluish-purple *O. arctobia*, and magenta *O. arctica*. There are arctic poppies nodding in the sun, bearberry, arctic cotton, and woolly lousewort. Cross over the Bailey bridge, and follow the road to the old townsite. Look for several mustards, dwarf fireweed, and other plants typical of old areas of human habitation.

Past the second bridge, you will find the road to Mount Pelly. Though the steep sides and windblown top of Mount Pelly have few flowers, check for the purple mountain saxifrage there. Check around the base for sheltered areas with little "gardens" of plants. The area to the north is home to one or two groups of musk oxen, and one usually can see small groups of caribou from the slopes. Nesting birds are *everywhere*, you will have to walk carefully to avoid stepping on nests. Keep your eyes open for fossils and seashells around Mount Pelly, but just look at what you find, and leave it behind for others to enjoy.

Head out of town past the North Warning System site (called Cam Main) and the airport, along the West Arm of the bay. This road extends to the popular summer camp area called the Gravel Pit. Here many of the Inuit residents of Cambridge Bay set up tents and live in the traditional way during the summer. All along this road, the flowers create a carpet. Arctic poppies, several species of buttercup, *Oxytropis arctobia*, and mountain avens are everywhere. At the Gravel Pit, the dwarf fireweed (Epilobium latifolium) covers the ground, growing in a rich mixture with *Astragalus alpinus*, the bulblet saxifrage, and yellow oxytrope.

Beyond the Gravel Pit, the road narrows to become an ATV path which passes the Japanese Monument (erected in memory of three Japanese students who lost their lives on the ocean). Look for old tent rings in this area.

The path continues to Long Point and follows a sandy beach past the Augustus Hills, good places to see musk oxen and arctic hares. The beach path leads to Starvation Cove, so named because an Inuit family starved to death there many years ago, when a shift in the caribou migration route took the deer another way. The trip to the cove takes three hours by ATV. Consider making this an overnight trip to ensure enough time to look at the flowers, watch wildlife, and fish.

For those limited to walking trips, you needn't go far out of town to enjoy the flowers. Follow any road, looking for a variety of habitats, and then examine each habitat in detail. Don't forget the edges of streams, ponds, and lakes, old campsites, marshy areas, open gravelly tundra, bird nesting areas, and the seashore; each has its own special flora.

The Arctic Coast Tourist Association operates a Visitor's Centre in Cambridge Bay. Call A.C.T.A. at (403) 920 - 7599 for information on guided day trips or overnight trips on Victoria Island, for information on accommodations in the area, or for the names of people in town interested in flowers.

Terrance Zeniuk

Gjoa Haven (Ursuqtuq)

Gjoa Haven is located on the southeast corner of King William Island, to the north of Chantrey Inlet, which is where the Back River enters the Arctic Ocean. The settlement, with a population of about 750, is at the head of a sandy inlet facing south. The flat tundra lowlands stretch away to the north, and the narrow bay provides shelter from storms. Numerous lakes and streams provide much marshy habitat.

Gjoa Haven is located on the fabled Northwest Passage, the long sought pathway through the ice-clogged straits between Rae Strait and the Queen Maud Gulf. The people of King William Island and the Boothia Peninsula to the east and Adelaide Peninsula to the south call themselves the Netsilingmiut, or "people of the seal". Though their lives are closely bound to the sea, they also hunt caribou and fish for arctic char.

This was an important area in the history of the search for the Northwest Passage. James Ross traveled to King William Island during the time he spent four years in the ice off the Boothia Peninsula (1829-1833). Dease and Simpson mapped the mainland coast to the south of King William Island in 1839, and ascertained that it was an island. And then, in the 1840s, Sir John Franklin and 129 men perished in the area. In fact, evidence of the ill-fated Franklin Expedition has been found on the site of Gjoa Haven and in the vicinity.

The Norwegian explorer, Roald Amundsen, entrusted his little herring boat, the *Gjoa*, to the ice in 1903, and took two years to negotiate the Passage. He spent two winters in the ice at Ursuqtuq, which he named "Gjoahavn" after his ship, calling it the "finest little harbor in the world". The local Netsilik people visited and traded with Amundsen, carried mail for him, and taught the explorers how to build snow houses.

During his summer on the island, Amundsen visited "Starvation Cove", where a group of men from the Franklin expedition perished. "Probably there is not another place in the world so abandoned and bare as this is in winter," he wrote. "There when summer comes and millions of flowers brighten up the fields... the waters gleam... where the birds swarm and brood with a thousand glad notes... a heap of bleached skeletons marks the spot where the remains of Franklin's brave crowd drew their last breath in that last act of that sad tragedy." (From "The Passage West", in Mowat, 1973, *Ordeal by Ice*.) Amundsen went on from Gjoa Haven in 1906 to become the first to complete the Northwest Passage.

The Hudson's Bay Company established a post at Gjoa Haven in 1927, and the Canalaska Co. had a post there during the late 1920s and early 1930s, encouraging the local people to trap arctic foxes for the fur trade. Since that time, the hamlet has grown, and, although many of the people still pursue a traditional lifestyle, an active arts and crafts industry flourishes, with soapstone carvings and unique appliqued wall hangings interpreting the wildlife of the area, and the traditional way of life.

In summer, the surrounding tundra glows with life, as tundra-nesting birds return to the land and the flowers burst into life. Gjoa Haven is so small that the visitor needs only to step out of town to be in contact with the tundra and its teeming life. Close to the settlement in the sandy areas, wild chamomile, bulblet saxifrage, mouse-eared chickweed, alpine crazyweed, several cinquefoils, and river beauty create a carpet of white, yellow, blue, and magenta.

In the wet areas, arctic cotton rings tundra ponds, or dots the land with white, the cuckoo flower (*Cardamine pratensis*) hides in the sedges, and buttercups lend a golden sparkle. Three species of poppies dance in the breezes, and mats of mountain avens lift their white parabolas to the welcome rays of the sun.

Several high arctic species overlap into this mid-arctic zone. There are several *Cerastium* species, and several *Stellaria, Ranunculus hyperboreus, Papaver cornwallensis* (the Cornwallis Island poppy), and several *Draba* and other mustards.

The Northwest Passage Territorial Park has been established in Gjoa Haven, and an interpretive trail provides a guide to several historical sites.

Signs and a printed trail guide provide background information. This trail is about 3 km in length, and wanders throughout the community and out onto the surrounding tundra. As you hike the trail, keep your eyes open for new flowers, especially in the low areas where water drains off the island. Check with the Hamlet office, or with Peter Akkitungaq of Opingak Tours for day trips by boat or ATV for wildlife viewing, rockhounding, fishing, or visits to historical sites, and for contacts in the community who are interested in the plants.

DND

Spence Bay (Taoyoak) (Taloyoak)

Located on the southwest coast of the Boothia Peninsula, Spence Bay is a fairly large body of water that zig-zags into the centre of the peninsula. It is surrounded by low rolling hills and numerous small lakes. The bay is free of ice for a few weeks in late summer, but quite a lot of the sea ice sometimes remains all summer in Ross and Rae Straits and the St. Roch Basin.

Spence Bay is located at the heart of the historic Northwest Passage; this area has been the site of many attempts to penetrate the ice and find a passage to the Pacific Ocean. The Boothia Peninsula was named by the explorer John Ross for Felix Booth, a patron of Ross' 1829-1833 expedition. Booth was a wealthy London distiller, the maker of Booth Gin, who provided support for Ross's expedition. Ross spent almost five years in the area, four winters in the ice on the eastern coast of the Boothia, ultimately abandoning his ship, the *Victory*, which became a treasure-trove of wood, iron, and other supplies for the Inuit residents of the area. He saved the lives of most of his men, however, and they fought their way in small boats almost to Bylot Island where they were picked up by a whaling ship. (See Mowat, 1976, for summary of Ross' story.) Ross also named Spence Bay, after a relative.

During the years of European exploration, mapping, and whaling, the area was sparsely populated, and the Netsilik people wandered over the land, responsive to the food supply and the seasons.

In the late 1920s a Hudson's Bay post was established at Fort Ross, a traditional Inuit camping site on southern Somerset Island. This location proved too difficult to service, due to constant sea ice, so in 1934, the H.B.C. began a complicated series of moves to relocate people from other areas onto better trapping grounds. People settled at Spence Bay in 1947. The population of the new post included Netsilingmiut from the Boothia and Simpson peninsulas, as well as people from the Cape Dorset area. Traditionally, the people who lived in this area depended heavily on ringed and bearded seals for sustenance.

The people of the Spence Bay area have also established quite a reputation as artisans and craftsmen, creating powerful carvings from soapstone and whalebone, as well as exquisite parkas and the unique Spence Bay "packing dolls." Local lichens were used to produce the dyes for the yarn designs that decorate the parkas and wall hangings.

Local writer Ernie Lyall established an international reputation with his book *An Arctic Man.* His son, Pat Lyall, operates Boothia Tours, taking visitors out on the sea ice and on overland wildlife viewing trips to see polar bears, seals, beluga and narwals, and (seasonally) caribou.

The area around Spence Bay is a low isthmus between the northern and southern halves of the Boothia Peninsula. Low rocky hills and huge boulders scattered over the land create the impression here that the great glaciers have only recently withdrawn from this land. Because of its isolation from the main continental land mass, the Spence Bay area has a flora more typical of the arctic islands than of the mainland. There are no alders, few willows, no cranberries, red bearberries (but there are black bearberries), or crowberries, but there are blueberries. Labrador tea is there, as is the white heather, but no rhododendron or bog rosemary. There are species that occur in the eastern arctic but do not occur in the rest of the central arctic.

In early summer, look for the tall spikes of arctic lousewort on fairly well-drained tundra. Early summer will also produce mustards — a couple of *Braya,* about four *Draba,* and the interesting arctic bladderpod with its unusual stellate (arranged in a starlike formation) hairs.

There are a lot of saxifrages, but many will not occur in large numbers. Look for the familiar prickly saxifrage on gravelly areas, and for the early-blooming purple mountain saxifrage on rocky outcrops. Bulblet saxifrage (*Saxifraga cernua*) may occur in association with the dwarf fireweed (*Epilobium latifolium*). Look for the snow saxifrage (*S. nivalis*) and yellow mountain saxifrage (*S. azioides*) on moist slopes, and for *Saxifraga foliolosa* and the small *Chrysosplenium tetrandrum* in marshy areas. *Saxifraga caespitosa* is a plant of the arctic islands, barely getting onto the mainland — look for this little tufted plant amongst the rocks or on gravelly areas. The unusual greenish purple flowers of *Saxifraga hieracifolia* are easily overlooked, but check out moist turfy habitats for this one; it's unusual in the rest of the area.

Two poppies occur in the area, the yellow arctic poppy, and the high arctic *Papaver cornwallisensis*, a dwarf species of wet gravelly areas. It is pale yellow, white, or pinkish yellow, and the leaves are less than 1 cm. long.

The chickweeds are well represented in the Spence Bay area. Of the mouse-eared chickweed group (*Cerastium*), there may be two species, *C. beeringianum* and *C. regelii* (which is a high arctic species rarely found on the mainland). In the star chickweed group (*Stellaria*), look for *S. humifusa* on islands or along the shore, *S. laeta* on wet tundra or moist rocky slopes, and the bluish-green *S. monantha*.

Only three legumes (pea family) cling to life here — the light blue *Astragalus alpinus*, the magenta-to-purple *Oxytropis arctobia*, and yellow *Oxytropis maydelliana*.

There are a few composites — a small pussy-toes (*Antennaria compacta*), mastodon flower, one dandelion (*Taraxacum lacerum*), and two daisies — the small *Chrysanthemum integrifolium*, and the larger wild chamomile (*Matricaria ambigua*) with its ferny leaves, living on the shore.

Finally, there are several later-blooming louseworts, the pink woolly lousewort, the yellow *Pedicularis capitata*, and peppermint-candy blooms of the *Sudetan lousewort* along little tundra streams.

Spence is a small community, and the botanizing is simply accomplished by walking out from town. If you've done your scanning from the aircraft on the way in, you'll have an idea of what areas you want to survey. The settlement of Spence Bay is located on a complex inlet with many arms. If you travel on the inlet by boat (or by skidoo in the early summer, when the snow is gone off the land), keep an eye out for interesting areas, the mouths of small streams, grassy swales, isolated small islands, old campsites or traditional hunting or fishing sites, etc. Any place where additional nutritive matter may have been deposited is a good place to stop and look for plants.

Check at the hamlet office for the names of people in town who are interested in the flowers, and work up an expedition. Remember, the summer days last almost 24 hours; someone who works during business hours may well be interested in looking at flowers well into the evening!

M. LaVigne

Pelly Bay (Arviligjuak)

Located on the west shore of the Simpson Peninsula (the east shore of Pelly Bay) at the mouth of the Kugajuk River, the small community of Pelly Bay (population, 325, in 1991) is one of the most isolated on the arctic coast. Its rocky terrain seems to have emerged only recently from beneath the ice of the great glaciers. In a starkly spectacular setting, the rugged land, abundant wildlife, and historic Inuit campsites combine to make it a memorable place to visit. Few outsiders live in the area, but the local people are proud of their land and their community, the first to be incorporated as a hamlet in 1973.

Although the bay is ice free for a few weeks in late summer, its mouth is blocked by pack ice the year round, and seagoing vessels cannot get to the community. All supplies must be flown in, and the cost of living here is among the highest in the north. Many people retain strong ties to the land, and still spend much of their year hunting caribou at inland camps, fishing in the rivers, and hunting seal on the sea ice.

The Pelly Bay area has long been occupied by the Netsilingmiut, or "people of the seal". It was a traditional seal hunting area, adjacent to good char fishing in the mouth of the Kugajuk River. The name Arviligjuak means "place of the bowhead whale", but none have been seen there for many years.

John Ross traded with the Netsilik people of the area, and wintered his ship north of Pelly Bay in 1829-1832. Dr. John Rae travelled to the area around Pelly Bay in 1854, in search of clues as to the fate fo the Franklin expedition. With the assistance of the local people, the story of the tragic loss of the entire expedition gradually emerged. The anthropologist Knud Rasmussen visited the area in 1923, and wrote about the Netsilingmiut in his extensive reports from the Fifth Thule Expedition.

Pelly Bay is named for Sir Henry Pelly, a 19th century governor of the Hudson's Bay Co., who organized the Dease and Simpson survey expeditions.

Two Roman Catholic priests have had great influence on the small community — Father Henry built the exquisite stone church in the late 1930s, and, with Father Vandevelde, who took his place, constructed a unique (and immense) cross of oil drums. The little stone church is now a museum housing Inuit artifacts.

During the early 1960s, the people of Pelly Bay worked with a highly skilled film crew to produce a series of films depicting the traditional way of life of the Netsilik people. These have been used extensively in Canada and the U.S., and account for many people's knowledge of the Inuit. Several of the films, without English narration, just a superb film record of daily life, have been used in sixth grade classes throughout the U.S. The people who starred in these films still live in Pelly, and remember the old ways. Many people still repair the old stone weirs in the mouth of the rivers, and fish there during the fall runs of arctic char.

The Pelly Bay area is extremely scenic, with high rocky hills, many gravelly streams, and many small lakes. Eider ducks, tundra swans, geese, loons, shorebirds, and snow buntings nest in the area. Tall inuksuit crown some of the ridges near town, and old tent rings and meat caches can be found.

Due to its isolation and the fact that the soil is extremely rocky, Pelly Bay is not exactly an oasis for flowers. It is difficult to determine whether the lack of collection records for the area is due to a lack of species, or a lack of collectors who have reported their finds in the literature! However, Pelly does have some species of flowers that are absent from the rest of the central arctic, representatives of a more typical "high arctic" flora.

The community is very small, so a summer visitor can simply walk out from the settlement on the land, looking for different habitats, and for the flowers typical of those habitats. There are sandy, gravelly, and rocky beaches, so you can hike along the shore, looking for typical beach plants. In the rocky areas, keep an eye out for moss campion and the purple mountain saxifrage, several buttercups, *Ranunculus hyperboreus, R. sabinei,* and *R. hyperboreus* (which is a high-arctic species that spills over into the low arctic). The white arctic heather is present at Pelly, but other typical heaths, such as bog rosemary, bearberry, and cranberry are absent.

Pelly has a much simpler flora, which makes the few species that are there much more precious. Look for *Ranunuculus nivalis* and *Saxifraga rivularis* near bird nesting sites, and for the prickly saxifrage on gravelly strandlines (old beaches elevated by glacial rebound). The yellow oxytrope (*Oxytropis maydelliana*) is the only common legume, although I'd suggest looking for *Oxytropis arctobia*, as it should be there.

If you find a pale yellow cinquefoil, it's likely *Potentilla hyparctica,* or, along the seashore, it may be *P. pulchella.* Walk along the river, and inland to some of the little tundra ponds, to see what plants you can find. Gabriel Nerlongajuk, of Netsilik Tours, offers day and overnight trips out of Pelly Bay. Check with him, or with the hamlet office for the names of people who are interested in the flowers.

A visit to Pelly Bay is, undoubtedly, a "discover it yourself" situation, as very little information on the plants of that area is currently available. If you visit, and do work out the plants, we'd certainly appreciate photos and/or a list of what is found! These can simply be sent to our publisher.

Glossary
Bibliography
Index

Glossary

ACIDIC (ROCKS): quartzite, granite, sandstone, or other rocks which do not react by producing bubbles when hydrochloric acid is applied. This means they do not contain calcium carbonate.

ALGA (ALGAE, pl.): group of lower, non-vascular plants, all containing chlorophyll. They range from unicellular forms to the giant kelps, and combine with a fungus to form a lichen.

ALKALOID: a nitrogen-containing organic compound insoluble in water, in this case, usually part of a poisonous factor in a plant.

ALPINE: typical of mountain areas, especially growing at or above timberline.

AMPHIBIOUS: adapted to life in water or on land.

AQUATIC: living, or at least rooted in water.

AROMATIC: a plant with a pungent (and often fragrant) smell.

ALTERNATE (BRANCHING, LEAF ATTACHMENT): (in leaves) having each leaf arising singly at a node; (referring to branches) having each branch arising by itself from one side of the main stem, without another branch immediately across from it. (Fig. A or No. 1)

ANTHER: the part of a stamen in which pollen is produced, most often an enlarged portion at the tip of the stamen. It is usually composed of two pollen sacs. (Fig. B or No. 2)

ARCTIC: (n.) term referring to the geographical area north of the treeline, extending all the way to the north pole; (adj.) of or having to do with the arctic regions of the world.

AXIL: the angle formed by the joining of one structure to another, most usually, between a branch and the stem, or a leaf and the stem. (Fig. A or No. 1)

AXIS: imaginary line indicating the portion of a plant from which a series of parts (leaves, branches, flowers) arises in a radial fashion; usually the stem of the plant or the rachis (main center stalk) of the flower cluster. (No. 1)

axil
alternate
axis
(1)

anthers
(2)

bilateral symmetry
irregular flower!
(3)

Figure A

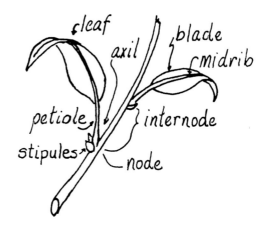

BASAL LEAVES: located at the base of a plant, close to the ground.

BILATERAL SYMMETRY: having two sides; type of arrangement in which a flower can be bisected in only one way in order to create two halves that are mirror images of each other. Used to refer to "irregular" flowers, such as those of orchids, legumes, louseworts, butterworts, and others, including the ray flowers of composites. *(No. 3)*

BLADE: the widest part of a leaf. *(Fig. A or No. 4)*

BOREAL: pertaining to the north, northern.

BOREAL FOREST: general term for the taiga biome, the great northern forest in which the dominant vegetational forms are coniferous trees.

BRACT: a specialized leaf from the axil of which a flower or flower stalk (such as the stalk of a flower cluster) arises. These usually do not have distinct petioles, and often are highly modified. *(No. 5)*

BUD: an undeveloped stem, leaf, or flower, often enclosed by specialized leaves called bud-scales. *(No. 6)*

BUD-SCALE: a modified and specialized leaf, often thin, dry, and papery, that covers and protects a leaf, branch, or flower bud. *(No. 6)*

blade

(4)

bract

(5)

buds
bud-scale

(6)

BULB: a short, often globular, underground organ composed in part of specialized leaves. Often functions as a food storage or reproductive (asexual) organ. An onion is an example of a bulb. *(No. 7)*

BULBIL: a bulb arising from a larger bulb, usually laterally, capable of developing into a new plant. Or, an asexual reproductive structure produced on the stem or branches of a plant, capable of developing into a new plant. *(No. 8)*

BULBLET: a "little bulb", term usually applied to the asexual reproductive structures produced by some plants in the axils of the leaves, or replacing the flowers. Also may refer to small bulbs that are produced by the division of a bulb. *(No. 8)*

CALYX: the outer set of flower parts, most often referring to the sepals. The calyx normally encloses the rest of the flower while it is in bud. It is usually green, but may be colored or petal-like. May be greatly reduced, or lacking entirely. *(Fig. B or No. 9)*

CALCAREOUS (ROCKS): rocks with a high percentage of calcium or magnesium carbonate cement, or minerals; usually refers to limestone rock, with a pH greater than 7, which produces bubbles when hydrochloric acid is applied.

CAMBIUM: in the woody plants, the layer between the outer bark and the inner wood.

CAPSULE: a dry, dehiscent (splitting open) fruit which develops from a compound ovary, and almost always contains two or more seeds.

CATKIN: a spike flower cluster made up of many highly modified (usually unisexual) flowers without petals, often appearing wormlike or drooping. *(No. 10)*

CHLOROPHYLL: the green pigment in plants that allows them (through photosynthesis) to convert water and carbon dioxide into carbohydrates in the presence of sunlight.

CIRCUMPOLAR: surrounding a pole, usually refers to geographic distribution around the north pole.

bulb

⑦

bulbil or bulblet

⑧

sepal

calyx

⑨

Figure B

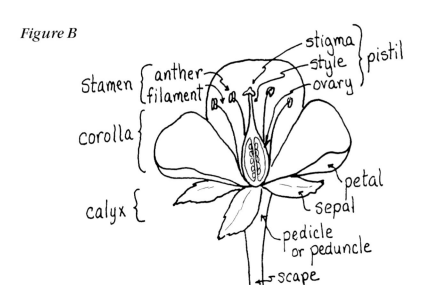

COROLLA: the second (and inner) set of segments of the perianth, usually the petals of the plant. *(Fig B or No. 11)*

CORYMB: a flat-topped raceme type of flower cluster. In this type of raceme, the axis is short, and the lower pedicels are long, placing all the flowers at approximately the same level, but they do not all arise at the same point, as in an umbel. *(No. 12)*

COTYLEDON: the embryonic leaf (or leaves) that appear when a seed germinates.

CRUSTOSE: lichen growth form in which the entire vegetative structure grows close to the substrate, like a coat of paint. There is no lower cortex in this type of lichen, because it is attached to the rock.

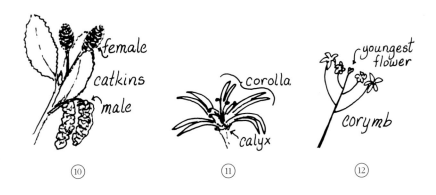

Figure C

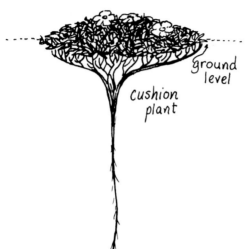

ground level

cushion plant

CUSHION PLANT: type of growth form in which the plant is pressed close to the ground in an aerodynamically efficient shape, allowing the wind to pass over it. *(Fig. C)*

CYME: a flat-topped (or convex) flower cluster in which the flowers at the centre bloom first. See "inflorescence". *(No. 13)*

DECIDUOUS: falling off at the end of a growing or blooming season. Usually refers to plants that drop their leaves at the end of the season.

DECUMBENT: prostrate except for the tips of the branches, which may point upward. *(No. 14)*

DEHISCENT: refers to a fruit or seed capsule which opens, usually by splitting along an axis.

DENE: term referring to the groups of native American people living south of the treeline and north of the prairies, Athapaskan peoples living in western Canada and Alaska.

DESSICATING: drying, removal of water by evaporation.

DICOT: a member of the Dicotyledonae, with two seed leaves emerging, flower parts in 4s, 5s, or multiples of those numbers, and branched veins in the leaves.

DIOECIOUS: bearing male (staminate) and female (pistillate) flowers on separate plants. Dioecious and monoecious refers to the condition of the *plant*, not the *flowers*.

DISK FLOWER (DISCOID FLOWER): the radially symmetrical tubular flowers of the composite family, usually central on the peduncle. *(Fig. E or No. 15)*

cyme

⑬

decumbent

⑭

disk flowers

ray flowers

⑮

DISTAL: refers to location on a plant; from the point of attachment outward. *(No. 16)*

DIURETIC: causes increased urination.

ENDEMIC: occurring only in a limited region, usually less than a continent. *Oxytropis arctobia* is endemic to the central arctic.

FOLIOSE: a leaflike lichen growth form, usually having both an upper and lower surface, may or may not be attached to the substrate.

FORAGE: food for herbivores.

FROND: the leaf of a fern. *(No. 17)*

FRUTICOSE: lichen growth form which is erect and bushy or hanging from a branch, usually attached only at one point. May grade into foliose — these terms for lichens are general ones.

FUNGUS (FUNGI, pl.): a general, non-botanical term used for several groups of plants that lack chlorophyll,reproduce by spores, and have a threadlike vegetative stage, although their fruiting bodies may assume a variety of shapes. Includes the smuts, molds, mildews, and shelf fungi, mushrooms and others.

GENUS (GENERA, pl.): name for a grouping of plants above the species level and below the family level, the name of which is the first word (capitalized) of the scientific name, a group of related species.

HABITAT: the type of place in which a plant usually grows, described in general terms, seabeach, marsh, heath tundra, etc.

HEAD: dense cluster of flowers, made up of several to many sessile or nearly sessile flowers crowded into a short axis, usually hemispherical. *(No. 18)*

HELMET: the hood-shaped upper petals of most of the Scrophulariaceae (louseworts). *(No. 19)*

INDIGENOUS: a native plant (as opposed to an introduced one).

INDUSIUM: (bladder fern) an outgrowth of the surface of the frond which wholly or partly covers the sori. *(No. 20)*

head

(18)

distal

(16)

frond

fiddlehead

(17)

helmet

lip

(19)

INFLORESCENCE: flower cluster, the way the flowers are arranged on the plant, includes spike, raceme, corymb, cyme, panicle, umbel, and head (of composite). *(No. 21)*

INTERNODE: on the stem of a plant, the section of stem between the nodes; visibly, between the places where leaves or branches arise. *(Fig A or No. 22)*

INUIT (pl.), INUK (singular): the people of North America north of the treeline, Eskimoes.

INUPIAT: Eskimoes of northern and northwestern Alaska.

INVOLUCRE, INVOLUCRAL BRACTS, INVOLUCRUM: cluster of overlapping modified leaves at the base of a flower cluster. *(Fig E or No. 23)*

IRREGULAR (FLOWER): flower that is not radially symmetrical, one that can be cut in one plane only to create two halves that are mirror images of each other. *(No. 3)*

KABLUNAK, KABLUUNA, QABLUNAAQ: the Inuit name for any non-Inuit.

KRUMMHOLZ: scrubby, stunted growth form often seen in woody plants of arctic or alpine areas. *(No. 24)*

LANCEOLATE: usually in reference to the shape of a leaf, shaped like a spear-head, longer than wide, and widest below the middle. *(No. 25)*

LATERAL: located on the side of or arising from the side of an organ, such as buds located on the sides (versus the tip) of a twig. *(No. 26)*

LEAF: photosynthetic organ of a plant, usually consisting of a relatively thin blade or blades, veins, and (usually, but not always) a petiole that attaches the leaf to the plant. Leaves may be highly modified, or even entirely absent. *(See Fig A)*

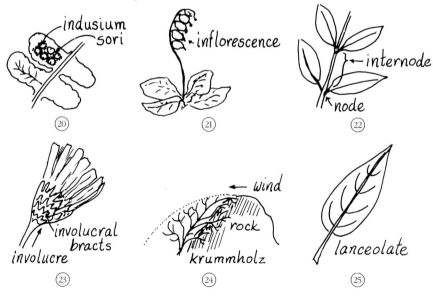

indusium
sori
(20)

inflorescence
(21)

internode
node
(22)

involucral
bracts
involucre
(23)

wind
rock
krummholz
(24)

lanceolate
(25)

Figure D

leaflet

LEAFLET: divisions of a leaf, each of which is a separate entity, all distal to the petiole. *(Fig. D)*

LIGULATE (FLOWER): one of the ray-flowers of a member of the composite family. *(Fig. E or No. 27)*

LINEAR (LEAVES): narrow leaves, with essentially parallel sides. *(No. 28)*

LOCULE: one of the cavities within an ovary, in which the seeds develop. *(No. 29)*

LOMENT: the seed pod of a member of the legume family composed of one-seeded articles. *(No. 30)*

MIDVEIN, MIDRIB: the central vein, or median rib of a leaf. *(Fig A)*

MONOCOT: group of plants germinating with one seed leaf; with flower parts in 3s or multiples of 3; with parallel leaf veins.

MONOECIOUS: having separate staminate (male) and pistillate (female) flowers on the same plant. A *plant* may be monoecious or dioecious; *flowers* are either unisexual (imperfect) or bisexual (perfect).

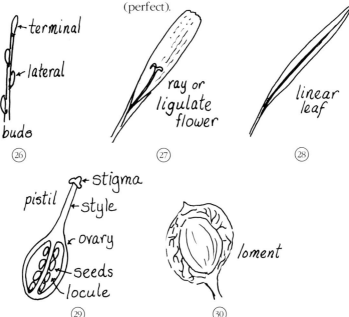

terminal

lateral

buds

㉖

ray or ligulate flower

㉗

linear leaf

㉘

pistil / stigma / style / ovary / seeds / locule

㉙

loment

㉚

MORPHS: "morphological form", a plant or flower exhibiting different (but inherited) color (or shape) characteristics, such as a white morph of the lupine.

NECTAR: sweet solution secreted by glands in many flowers; attracts pollinators.

NECTARY: gland or set of glands that secrete nectar, and the structure that contains the glands or stores the nectar.

NON-CALCAREOUS (ROCKS): rocks that do not contain a high percentage of calcium or magnesium carbonate. These rocks do not bubble when hydrochloric acid is applied.

NODE: place on the stem from which leaves or branches (and sometimes, roots) arise. *(No. 31)*

OPPOSITE (BRANCHING, LEAF ATTACHMENT): branches or leaves attached opposite each other on the stem of a plant, in pairs as opposed to alternating. *(No. 31)*

OVARY: the basal part of a pistil, usually expanded, in which the ovules are borne, and in which the seeds develop. *(No. 29 and Fig. B)*

OVULE: in plant sexual reproduction, the female cell before fertilization. After fertilization (joining of the male reproductive material) and development, the ovule becomes a seed.

PALMATE: radiating from a single point, like fingers from the palm of the hand; also called digitate. (VENATION: refers to the veins in a leaf blade, radiating from a point where the petiole joins the blade) *(No. 33)*

PALMATELY COMPOUND (LEAVES): three or more leaflets radiating from a common point of attachment, as in the lupines, some buttercups, some cinquefoils. *(No. 32)*

PANICLE: flower cluster or inflorescence with branches on branches, longer than it is wide. *(No. 34)*

PAPPUS: hairs, scales, or bristles growing as an outgrowth of the seed of a composite. Used to refer to the silky bristles the flowerheads of *Saussurea*. *(No. 35)*

opposite leaves
node
(31)

palmately compound leaf
(32)

palmate venation
(33)

panicle
(34)

PARASITIC: plant that derives its food and moisture entirely from another living plant; usually does not kill host plant.

PEDICLE: stalk of each flower in a flower cluster/inflorescence. *(Fig. B or No. 36)*

PEDUNCLE: the part of the stem that bears a flower cluster or a single flower, usually identified by being leafless or with bracts only.

PERIANTH: in a flower, the corolla and calyx (petals and sepals) considered together, or one or the other if one is absent. *(No. 37)*

PERIANTH BRISTLES: (in arctic cotton) modification of the petals and sepals to form slender fibers, which make up the "heads" of arctic cotton (see *Eriophorum* in species accounts).

PETIOLE: stalk-like portion of an ordinary leaf, connecting it with the stem of the plant; often has (especially in woody plants) a slightly expanded base. *(No. 38)*

PHOTOSYNTHESIS: the process by which green plants convert sunlight and carbon dixoide into carbohydrates.

PINNATE: branching off a single center vane, branches, lobes, leaflets, or veins arranged on two sides of a center rachis. *(No. 39)*

PINNATE VENATION: leaf veins arising from a center vein, resembling the arrangement of a feather. *(No. 39)*

PINNATELY COMPOUND: in leaflet arrangement within a compound leaf, leaflets that arise off the sides of a center rachis, such a those of *Hedysarum, Oxytropis,* and some of the cinquefoils, buttercups, and mustards. *(No. 40)*

PINNATIFID: usually used for fronds or leaves, leaf with lobes, clefts, or divisions arranged pinnately (as the veins of a feather). *(No. 40)*

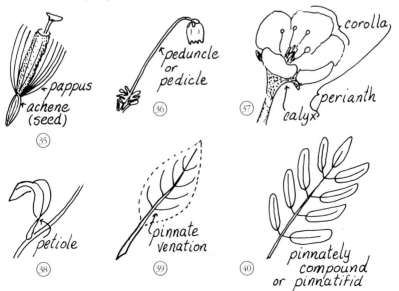

PISTIL: the female organ(s) of the flower, consisting of the ovary, style, and stigma; the structures of the flower that receive the pollen. *(Fig B and No. 41)*

PISTILLATE (FLOWERS): flowers which bear only the female parts, and lack the stamens; they do not produce pollen, but only receive it.

POD: a general term for a dry fruit in which the seeds are borne, generally used to refer to members of the pea family.

POLLEN: the male genetic material of the plant, borne within the anther of the stamen.

POLLINIUM (POLLINIA, pl.): in the orchids, the small masses of pollen which are borne together, and detach from the plant together.

PROCUMBENT: prostrate or trailing over the ground, but not rooting where the nodes touch the ground. *(No. 42)*

PROSTRATE: lying flat on the ground, seabeach sandwort, seaside mertensia, for example. *(No.42)*

PUBESCENT: bearing hairs on the surface.

RACEME: flower cluster or inflorescence with unbranched central axis and lateral flowers, each on a separate pedicel, lowest blooming first. *(No. 43)*

RACHIS: the axis (centre stem or vane) of the inflorescence, or of a compound leaf. *(No. 43)*

RADIAL SYMMETRY: in reference to the shape of a flower, a flower that, wherever it is cut (vertically through the centre) would produce two halves that are mirror images of each other. *(No. 44)*

RANGE: geographical area in which a plant is found.

RAY FLOWER: strap-like marginal flowers in the composite family, also known as ligulate flowers. *(Fig E)*

RECEPTACLE: the apex of a pedicel or single-flowered peduncle which bears the floral parts; in the composites, the expanded apex of the pedicle on which the flowers are inserted. *(Fig E)*

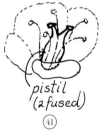

pistil
(2 fused)

(41)

procumbent
or prostrate

(42)

rachis

raceme

(43)

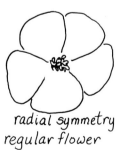

radial symmetry
regular flower

(44)

Figure E

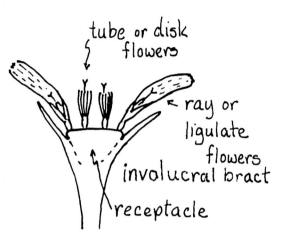

tube or disk flowers

ray or ligulate flowers

involucral bract

receptacle

RHIZOME: horizontal stems of a plant, located underground, which produce roots, and also aerial stems. Can be an important method of asexual reproduction. *(No. 45)*

ROSETTE: cluster of leaves crowded close together, often at the base of the plant, as a basal rosette. *(See Fig. F)*

SCAPE: flower stalk (leafless or with bracts only) arising directly from the ground or from a short stem. *(No. 46)*

SCIENTIFIC NAME: the latinized name by which an organism is recognized the world over. It consists of two (or sometimes more) terms, the genus name and the specific epithet. In *Arnica alpina*, the genus is *Arnica*, and the specific epithet is *alpina*. The species is *Arnica alpina*. Scientific names follow rules set forth by the International Commission on Botanical Nomenclature. The genus name is always capitalized, and the specific epithet is not (although, if it was derived from a person's name, it used to be capitalized in botanical nomenclature only). The scientific name is italicized if possible, and underlined if italics are not available in the typeface being used. Confused? You're not alone. Just remember that the scientific name is a name that is recognized the world over, by us, the Russians, Chinese, Arabs, etc., and that it is always written in Roman orthography (the type of letters we recognize) as opposed to being written in Cyrillic script, Arabic, or syllabics.

SEED: a ripened ovule.

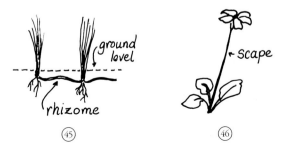

ground level

rhizome

⁴⁵

scape

⁴⁶

Figure F

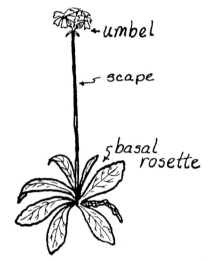

SEPALS: modified leaves, segments of the calyx, usually green and thicker than the petals, enclosing the flower bud. The sepals may be "petaloid", of a color and texture like the petals. *(Fig. B or no. 47)*

SERRATE: usually refers to the edge of the leaf, toothed along the margin, with teeth directed forward, toward the tip. *(No. 48)*

SESSILE: without a stalk, usually a flower or leaf attached directly to the stem, without a pedicel, petiole, peduncle. *(No. 49)*

SILICLE: the short, wide, flat seedpod (a short form of silique) characteristic of some of the mustards. *(No. 50)*

SILIQUE: seed pod of the mustards, elongating as it develops, and composed of a central thin partition (the "replum"), and two valves, which separate from the replum to release the seeds. "Silique" usually refers to the longer pods, and "silicle", to the short fat flat ones. *(No. 51)*

SORUS (SORI, pl.): in the ferns, a cluster of spore cases on a frond or fertile stalk. These are the dark dots on the underside of the fertile fronds of ferns. *(No. 20)*

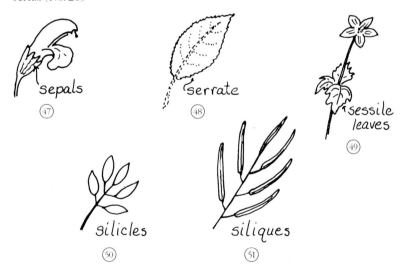

SP.: abbreviation for species, refers to the scientific name.

SPP.: abbreviation for "a group of species", as when one is referring to several species of saxifrage, using *Saxifraga* spp. means the entry refers to more than one species of saxifrage.

SSP.: abbreviation for "subspecies", when referring to several subspecies of a particular species, such as *Oxytropis deflexa* ssp., which refers to several varieties of *O. deflexa.*

SPATULATE: in reference to leaf shape, flat or broadened toward a rounded tip. *(No. 52)*

SPECIES: subdivision of a genus; a group of plants that interbreed freely, and have many characteristics in common. See "specific epithet".

SPECIFIC EPITHET: the second name in the scientific name of an organism, in *Arnica alpina,* "alpina" is the specific epithet, *Arnica alpina* is the species name. In referring to the alpine arnica, it would be incorrect to refer to it as "alpina", because this could refer to *Draba alpina,* or any other "alpina". One must use a combination of the genus name and the specific epithet. The genus name can be abbreviated within the same short section where it is obvious one is discussing the members of that particular genus. See "scientific name."

SPIKE: term for a flower cluster in which sessile flowers are arranged on a long stem, with the bloom beginning at the bottom. *(No. 53)*

SPORANGIUM (SPORANGIA, pl.): a spore case.

SPORE: a single-celled asexual reproductive unit of the non-flowering plants (fungi, ferns, horsetails, etc.).

STAMEN: the male organ of a flower, bearing the pollen on an anther. *(Fig. B or No. 54.)*

STAMINATE: male flowers, those that have stamens, but lack pistils.

STAMINODIA: odd sterile stamen-like structures alternating with the true stamens in *Parnassia.*

STANDARD (OF PEA FLOWER): the uppermost petal (actually, two petals, fused) of the flowers of the Leguminosae or pea family. *(No. 55)*

spatulate

(52)

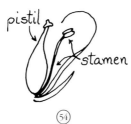

spike

(53)

pistil

stamen

(54)

standard

(55)

STELLATE HAIRS: groups of hairs all arising from a common base, spread out to form a star shape, as in *Lesquerella arctica*.

STIGMA: the portion of a pistil that receives the pollen. *(Fig B and No. 58)*

STIPULE: a modified leaf which is located at the base of a leaf or petiole, often paired, varying in structure from papery to almost leaflike. *(Fig. A or No. 56)*

STOLON: horizontal branch that arises near the base of a plant, and is capable of taking root at its nodes or apex. *(No. 57)*

STOLONIFEROUS: plant producing stolons.

STRANDLINES: old beaches elevated above current sea level by glacial rebound.

STROBILUS (STROBILI, pl.): cluster of modified leaves arranged on an axis in a conelike structure which bears the spores; the "head" of a fertile frond of horsetail.

STYLE: the stalk of the pistil, which connects the ovary and the stigma. *(Fig. B or No. 58)*

SUBSTRATE: the base upon which an organism lives, such as the soil, rocks, other plants, etc.

SUCCULENT: having fleshy stems or leaves that store water.

SYMBIOSIS: two dissimilar organisms living together in intimate association, which may or may not be mutually beneficial.

TAIGA (BIOME): the huge area of primarily coniferous forest in the

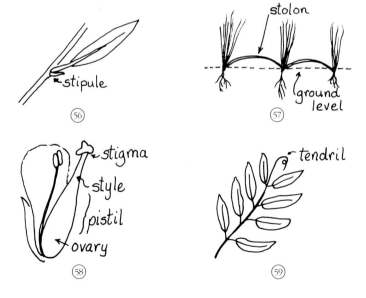

Northern Hemisphere south of the tundra, dominated by spruces and firs.

TENDRIL: a part of a stem or leaf modified to serve as a holding organ, often spiraling around a support to provide a grip. *(No. 59)*

TERMINAL: located at the end or apex of a structure, such as a terminal bristle in gentian flowers, or terminal bud on a branch.

THALLUS: a plant body lacking true leaves, stems, roots, or flowers, as in lichens, algae, liverworts, etc.

TUBE FLOWER: another term for the disk flowers of the composites. *(Fig. E)*

TUNDRA (BIOME): the large circumpolar area north of the treeline, characterized by dwarfed vegetation, a lack of coniferous trees, and underlain by continuous permafrost, also can be used for the habitat type above the treeline and below the zone of perpetual snow on mountains.

TUSSOCK: a tuft of grass or grasslike plants like the sedges, often a thick bundle the size of a man's head, attached to the ground by a tough and flexible neck. *(No. 60)*

TUSSOCK TUNDRA: type of tundra consisting of acre upon acre of sedge tussocks, usually located on flat, poorly drained land or gentle slopes; the most diabolical hiking areas known to man.

UMBEL: flower cluster shaped like an umbrella, in which all the flowers arise from one point. *(No. 61)*

VASCULAR PLANT: large group of plants having a network of tubes that conduct water, nutrients, and mineral solutions through the tissues of the plant. Vascular plants include the ferns and seed-bearing plants, but not the fungi, mosses, liverworts, algae, lichens, etc., which are termed "non-vascular plants".

VISCID: sticky.

WHORLED: three or more structures arising at the same node, or at the same level on an axis. Usually refers to leaf arrangement. *(No. 62)*

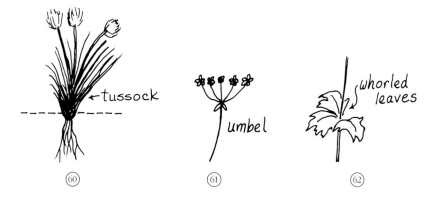

←tussock

umbel

whorled leaves

60

61

62

Bibliography

Alvin, Kenneth L. 1977.
The Observer's Book of Lichens.
Frederick Warne, London.

Arno, Stephen F. and Hammerly, Ramona P. 1984.
Timberline, Mountain and Arctic Forest Frontiers.
The Mountaineers, 306 2nd Ave. W., Seattle, WA. 98119, and Douglas & McIntyre Ltd., 1615 Venables St., Vancouver, B.C. V5L 2H1

Britton, Max E. 1966. Vegetation of the Arctic Tundra.
IN, Hansen, Harry. 1966. **Arctic Biology.**
Oregon State University Press, Corvallis, Ore.

Chung, In-Cho. 1984.
The Arctic and Rockies as Seen by a Botanist Pictorial. Privately published, In-Cho Chung, 1251 Towncrest Rd., Williamsport, Pa. 17701.

Clark, Lewis J. and Trelawny, J. 1975.
Lewis Clark's Field Guide to Wildflowers of the Mountains in the Pacific Northwest.
Gray's Publishing Limited, Sidney, B.C.

Coombes, Allen J. 1985.
Dictionary of Plant Names.
Timber Press, Portland, Oregon.

Domico, Terry. 1979.
Wild Harvest, Edible Plants of the Pacific Northwest.
Hancock House Publishers, 19313 Zero Ave., Surrey, B.C. V3S 5J9

Foersom, Th., Kapel, F.O., and Svarre, O. 1982.
Nunatta Naasui/ Gronlands flora i farver. (Flowers of Greenland) Kalaallisut suliarinera Isak Heilmann. Pilersuiffik.

Francis, Daniel. 1986.
Discovery of the North; the Exploration of Canada's Arctic.
Hurtig Publishers, Edmonton.

Gray, David R. 1987.
The Muskoxen of Polar Bear Pass.
(For National Museum of Natural Sciences, National Museums of Canada) Fitzhenry & Whiteside, 195 Allstate Parkway, Markham, Ont. L3R 4T8

Grey-Wilson, Christopher. 1981.
The Alpine Flowers of Britain and Europe.
Collins, St. James's Place, London.

Haber, Eric. 1986.
Adaptations of Arctic Plants, and, Flora of the Circumpolar Arctic.
IN, Sage, Bryan. 1986. **The Arctic & Its Wildlife.** Facts on File Publications, N.Y., N.Y.

Hall, Ed (Editor). 1989.
People & Caribou in the Northwest Territories.
G.N.W.T., Dept. of Renewable Resources. Available from: Dept. of Culture & Communications, Publications and Production Division, P.O. Box 1320, Yellowknife, N.W.T. X1A 2L9

Heller, Christine A. 1985.
Wild Edible and Poisonous Plants of Alaska.
Cooperative Extension Service, Publication No. A-00028, University of Alaska.

Houston, C. Stuart. 1984.
Arctic Ordeal; The Journal of John Richardson, Surgeon-Naturalist with Franklin, 1820-1822.
McGill-Queen's University Press, Kingston and Montreal.

Hulten, E. 1968.
Flora of Alaska and Neighboring Territories.
Stanford Univ. Press, Stanford, Ca.

Irons, Joanne. 1987.
"Vascular Plants Checklist for Coppermine, N.W.T."
Unpublished list.

Johnson, Karen L. 1987.
Wildflowers of Churchill and the Hudson Bay Region.
Manitoba Museum of Man and Nature, Winnipeg, Manitoba.

Kingsbury, John M. 1964.
Poisonous Plants of the United States and Canada.
Prentice-Hall, Inc., New Jersey.

Krochmal, Arnold and Connie. 1973.
A Guide to the Medicinal Plants of the United States.
Quadrangle, The New York Times Book Co., 10 E. 53 St., N.Y., N.Y. 10022.

Lopatka, S., Ross, D., and Stoesz, R. 1990.
Northwest Territories Data Book 1990/91.
Outcrop Ltd., The Northern Publishers. Box 1350, Yellowknife, N.W.T. X1A 2N9.

McGregor, Cathy, Gilmour, Margy, and Kindt, Don. 1985.
Elementary Science Primary and Intermediate Program Guides, and **Plants, A Language Development Unit.**
School Programs, Dept. of Education, G.N.W.T.

Mowat, Farley. 1960.
Ordeal by Ice; The Search for the Northwest Passage.
McClelland & Stewart Ltd., Toronto.

Porsild, A.E. 1951.
"Plant Life in the Arctic."
Reprint from **Canadian Geographical Journal**, March 1951.
National Museums of Canada, Ottawa.

Porsild, A.E. 1973.
Illustrated Flora of the Canadian Arctic Archipelago
(1957). Bulletin No. 146. National Museum of Natural Sciences, National Museums of Canada, Ottawa. (No longer available.)

Porsild, A.E. and Cody, W.J. 1980.
Vascular Plants of Continental Northwest Territories, Canada. National Museum of Natural Sciences, National Museums of Canada, Ottawa, Canada.

Savile, D.B.O. 1972.
Arctic Adaptations in Plants.
Monograph No. 6, Canada Dept. of Agriculture, Research Branch. Was available from: Information Division, Canada Dept. of Agriculture, Ottawa, Ont. K1A 0C7.

Schofield, Janice J. 1989.
Discovering Wild Plants, Alaska, Western Canada, the Northwest.
Alaska Northwest Books, GTE Discovery Publications, Inc., 22026 20th Ave. S.E., Bothell, WA. 98021.

Shuttleworth, Floyd S. and Zim, Herbert S. 1967.
Mushrooms and other Non-flowering Plants.
Golden Press, N.Y. and Western Publishing Co., Inc., Racine, Wisconsin.

Trelawny, John G. 1983.
Wildflowers of the Yukon and Northwestern Canada Including Adjacent Alaska.
Sono Nis Press, 1745 Blanshard St., Victoria, B.C. V8W 2J8

Vitt, D.H., Marsh, J.E., and Bovey, R.B. 1988.
Mosses, Lichens & Ferns of Northwest North America.
Lone Pine Publishing, 414, 10357 - 109 St., Edmonton, Alberta, T5J 1N3, or Univ. of Washington Press, P.O. Box 50096, Seattle, WA. 98145-5096.

Walker, Marilyn. 1984.
Harvesting the Northern Wild.
Outcrop, The Northern Publishers, Yellowknife, N.W.T.

Weber, William A. 1988.
Colorado Flora: Western Slope.
Colorado Associated University Press, Boulder, Colorado 80309.

Welsh, Stanley L. 1974.
Anderson's Flora of Alaska and Adjacent Parts of Canada.
Brigham Young Univ. Press, Provo, Utah.

Wilkinson, Douglas. 1970.
The Arctic Coast. The Illustrated Natural History of Canada.
Natural Science of Canada Ltd., 58 Northline Rd., Toronto.

Young, Steven B. 1989.
To the Arctic; An Introduction to the Far Northern World.
Wiley Science Editions, John Wiley & Sons, Inc., N.Y., N.Y.

Zoltai, S.C., Karasiuk, D.J., and Scotter, G.W. 1980.
A Natural Resource Survey of the Bathurst Inlet Area, Northwest Territories.
Parks Canada, Ottawa.

Zwinger, Ann H. and Willard, Beatrice E. 1972.
Land Above the Trees; A Guide to American Alpine Tundra.
Harper & Row, Publishers, Inc., 10 East 53rd St., New York, N.Y. 10022.

Index

O

okpeet 48
oleaster family 126
Onagraceae 152
orchid family 40
Orchidaceae 40
Oxyria digyna 58
Oxytropis arctica 122
Oxytropis arctobia 122
Oxytropis hyperborea 120
Oxytropis maydelliana 120

P

paintbrush 168
painted cup 168
Pallas' wallflower 68
Papaver cornwallisensis 86
Papaver hultenii 86
Papaver radicatum 84
Papaver keelei 86
Papaveraceae 84
Parnassia kotzebuei 98
Parnassia palustris 98
Parrya arctica 68
pea family 114
Pedicularis 170
Pedicularis arctica 172, 174
Pedicularis capitata 172
Pedicularis flammea 172
Pedicularis labradorica 174
Pedicularis lanata 174
Pedicularis lapponica 172
Pedicularis sudetica 176
Petasites sagittatus 190
Petasites frigidus 190
Pinguicula sp. 150
Pinguicula villosa 150
Pinguicula vulgaris 150
pink family 60
Plumbaginaceae 144
Poa sp. 34
Polygonaceae 58
Polygonum viviparum 58
poppy family 84
Populus balsamifera 48
Populus tremuloides 48
Potentilla egedii 90
Potentilla fruticosa 90

Potentilla nivea 92
Potentilla palustris 92
Potentilla rubricaulis 92
prickly saxifrage 106
primrose family 162
Primula egaliksensis 162
Primula stricta 162
Primulaceae 162
purple bladder-campion 62
purple mountain saxifrage 108
pussy-toes 182
pygmy aster 184
pygmy buttercup 84
pygmy flower sp. 164
Pyrola grandiflora 158
Pyrola secunda 158
Pyrolaceae 158

R

ragworts 194
Ranunculaceae 78
Ranunculus gmelinii 82
Ranunculus hyperboreus 82
Ranunculus pedatifidus 84
Ranunculus pygmaeus 84
Ranunculus sabinei 82
Ranunculus sulphureus 82
red bearberry 132
Rhizocarpon geographicum 24
Rhododendron lapponicum 134
Richardson's anemone 78
Richardson's milk-vetch 116
river beauty 154
rock cranberry 138
rock-jasmine 162
rock tripe 22
Rosaceae 86
rose family 86
Rubus chamaemorus 94

S

Salicaceae 48
Salix alaxensis 52
Salix herbacea 52
Salix reticulata 50
Salix sp. 48
Saussurea angustifolia 192
Saxifraga aizoides 110

CM   INCHES

16

        6

14

        5

12

        4

10

8

        3

6

        2

4

        1